Be A Thermostat

Nola C. Veazie, Ph.D.

To order additional copies, please contact us.
BookSurge, LLC
www.booksurge.com
1-866-308-6235
orders@booksurge.com

Be A Thermostat

Be A Thermostat

CONTENTS

ACKNOWLEDGEMENT

Be A Thermostat acknowledges that the spirit of God leads you into the knowledge of all truth; the same spirit reveals the things that hinder your growth and stops you from achieving your purpose in life. This is a resource for every person who is currently paralyzed by bitterness and resentment.

INTRODUCTION

Unregulated anger, like a veil, descends on the human soul and covers God's spiritual light that shines through you. It blocks God's revelation of the authentic you, instead uncovering the potential evil that is in all of us. This out-of-control anger ticks like a time-bomb ready to explode at any given moment; the person holding the detonating device is not you. Allowing yourself to be consumed by this explosion of anger is like surrendering to the terrorist who tries to create fear and chaos, changing your very essence into an evil that will later destroy you.

Since the fall of mankind there has been an increase in violence, riots, rebellion, and hostilities as a result of man's inappropriate display of anger. From the Old Testament account of Abel's death at the hand of his brother Cain to 21st century drive-by shootings, unregulated anger has been a problem and continues to escalate into violent behavior that produces deadly outcomes. God's word cautions us not to allow our anger to escalate into negative behaviors ("be angry and sin not") and to manage our angry feelings through communication and forgiveness before sunset ("do not let the sun go down on your wrath").

Dealing with and accepting feelings of anger is difficult for many people. Hearing the word *ANGER* registers in the brain as something negative, it conjures images of warning, danger, and alert sings. These images soon creep in to your daily lives, turning your darkest and deepest fears into a deadly reality. Although there has been much information disseminated about anger and how to deal with it, people continue to experience its negative effects.

A number of people believe that anger is evil or bad and they should avoid it at all cost; some believe that anger hurts people that nice people don't get angry, and if they allow themselves to feel anger they may lose control over their emotions. Teachings we receive from our family of origin, our local churches, and our own experiences reinforce these myths about anger.

Be a thermostat: Regulate your anger, uses scripture and researched information to challenge your belief about anger and provide you with anecdotes that will allow you to explore your own emotions; it motivates you to meditate on God's word about anger and recognize that even though God created you with the capacity to experience anger, he has placed in you the ability to regulate it. This book also shows you that you have a choice between being a thermostat (using your anger as energy to resolve problems) or a thermometer (reacting to environmental cues, to people, and your own feelings).

Chapter 1

ANGER

"Be angry and do not sin, do not let the sun go down on your wrath"

(Ephesians 4:26)

Anger can be defined as something people fear and a feeling or experience that should be avoided at all cost. Some dictionaries define anger as a hostile feeling because of opposition, a feeling of extreme displeasure, hostility, indignation, or exasperation toward someone or something while experts in the field of anger management see it as a normal emotion or feeling experienced by all of us as a reaction to a stimulus (person or situation). What does the creator say about anger? God's word simply says, "be angry and sin not." The bible shows anger as a normal emotion displayed by God, an emotion you will feel, but does not have to lead to inappropriate behaviors that results in negative outcomes.

Regardless of the definition, we know that the outcome of uncontrolled anger can be devastating to the individual, family members, and society. In recent years, the media has brought the problem to the forefront; the nightly news show incident after incident of road-rage, domestic violence (20% of women presenting with injuries at emergency rooms were victims of domestic violence), family violence (1 in 5 of all aggravated assaults reported to the police were aggravated assaults in the home), and an overall disintegration of people's ability to deal appropriately with their anger.

On April 20, 1999, we were all horrified as we watched the news about the Columbine shootings. The thought of two students killing fellow classmates and a teacher both scared and amazed us. Our perplexity and fear increased even more when we heard the story about the Washington snipers randomly killing unsuspecting victims in at least three States. Unfortunately, these were not isolated cases. Anger related crimes have been around throughout history, some less prominent, like the former refinery station employee in Texas (April 1995) who killed the owner and the owner's wife before turning the gun on himself. These and other known cases are daily reminders that uncontrolled anger can be devastating.

Anger, however, is not a phenomenon of the 21st century; it dates way back to the Old Testament. The inappropriate expression of anger leading to violence was first documented in the book of Genesis, when Cain murdered Abel because of jealousy: Genesis 4:5-8....And Cain was very angry, and his countenance fell; now Cain talked with Abel his brother; and it came to pass, when they were in the field, that Cain rose against Abel his brother and killed him.

Unregulated and inappropriately expressed anger not only poses an external threat to society, but also poses an internal threat to the individual who is controlled by it. When you allow your anger to get out of control, it becomes an emotional trap that captures and confines you like a small animal, which later attacks those around. The effects of uncontrolled anger, like tentacles, often reach deep into the soul causing spiritual numbness. Proverbs 22:24-25 tells us not to make a friendship with an angry person unless we learn their angry ways, thus "setting a trap for our souls."

Points for discussion:

The bible makes many references to anger and points out that it is a normal feeling we experience; however, it warns us against the negative effects of unregulated anger. Answer the following questions about your anger and write down your answers for later discussion.

1. What is your definition of anger?
2. What do you consider unregulated anger?
3. How do you monitor your level of anger?
4. On a scale from 1-10 where is the level of your anger?
5. What does the verse in Ephesians 4:26 mean to you?
6. When the book of Proverbs cautions against making friendships with angry people, what does it imply? Proverbs 22:24
7. Is anger a sin?
8. List the physical changes you experience when you are angry (i.e. increased heart rate, muscle tension)
9. List the emotional changes you experience when you are angry (i.e. increased anxiety)
10. List the behavioral changes you experience when you are angry (i.e. hitting, pacing)

Pay attention to physical response to emotion.

Angry people hurt people

No one can make you feel inferior without your consent
      —Eleanor Roosevelt

Increasingly, you are faced with angry people or situations that cause you to react with anger. The workplace has become a battlefield in which you arm yourself for battle against backstabbers, harsh words from co-workers or the boss, and abusive language in the office. Your home, once your sanctuary from the storm, has become an extension of the battlefield, because of verbal or physical abuse. At times there seems to be no place in the world to hide from anger or angry people.

An inappropriate expression of anger doesn't always lead to killing, but always leaves emotional casualties in its path. Unregulated or unmanaged anger causes the individual to inflict pain on others by using harsh words that can escalate to verbal abuse; anger can lead people to say things to loved one's they wish they could take back, or act in a way that inflicts pain on others. According to the book of Proverbs, an angry person stirs up strife (i.e., they create a hostile atmosphere, full of drama) and one who is furious is full of transgressions (breaks the law or command).

Before you stick your nose in the air about the way others deal with their anger, it is important to note that we all get angry. Unfortunately, many of us can identify with the inappropriate expression of anger. Remember when that rude person cut in line in front of you in the store? If someone could hear your internal dialogue, it might sound something like this: I should give him or her a piece of my mind or maybe I should push him/her with my cart, I bet that will help him or her along. Think about the person who cut in front of you on the highway only to drive 55 mph? Do you recall the way you handled that situation?

Anger is not bad, it is an emotion we all experience and a universal feeling expressed in many ways by different people. Although by itself it is not dangerous, the way we learn to deal with and express our anger can be. The expression of our anger is often fueled by cognitive distortions (i.e., our ability to turn an ant hill into a mountain) that intensify the feeling and lead to hostility and aggression. Irrational thinking about the situation and negative appraisals about the person inflames the issue further, leading to negative outcomes, such as broken relationships or physical and psychological problems.

Anger has a way of clouding your judgment and coloring your perceptions (not in a very nice color). When you are angry, you interpret people's actions and words more negatively (i.e. "Joe said he doesn't like the color blue, I know he was probably talking about my favorite blue shirt"). You also perceive their intentions to be more hostile than they really are ("he just wanted to ruin my day"). Coupled with irrational thinking (i.e. people like Joe think they are better than me), the myths you learned about anger (i.e. people make me angry) perpetuate the cycle of shame, guilt, and negative behaviors that can keep you from enjoying a good relationship with others and most importantly with God.

What myths do you believe about anger? Some people believe that anger hurts people; the truth is people hurt people. They become hurt and disappointed when life brings lemons instead of lemon flavored smoothies; frustrated, they turn their anger towards others. For example, Cain probably expected God's response to his offering to be one of excitement and approval because his job of tilling the ground was important. His internal conversation was probably, *wait until God sees what I did, he will most likely pat me on the back and tell me how much better my offering is than my brother Abel's*. God's response was much different than Cain's expectation (Genesis 4:2).

Those of us familiar with the story know that God looked at Abel's heart and not his offering, valuing Abel's gift more than He did Cain's. Cain's natural response to perceived rejection was hurt, disappointment, and anger. Cain was unable to see that God wanted him to give up anger and take on a humble spirit. And the Lord asked Cain "Why are you angry? If you do well, will you not be accepted and if you do not do well, sin lies at the door." God warned Cain that sin's (in this case his unregulated anger) desire was to overtake him, but he should not allow it; instead, he should rule over it.

Sometimes you may allow anger to rule over rational thinking, leading you to hurt someone; Cain allowed anger to seduce him into killing his brother. What will you allow your anger to do? Many of you can recall a time that you did something nice for someone, only to see your good deed met with criticism or an unappreciative gesture. Their criticism of your deed then caused you to feel hurt and disappointed, leading you to react in a way that hurts them back. Your primary goal then becomes, inflicting pain on the person who hurt you.

Unfortunately, angry people do not always hurt the person they are angry with; they displace their anger and take it out on someone more vulnerable instead. The victim of bullying may not have the courage to retaliate against the bully, but is able to regain power by victimizing someone less powerful. There are many examples of people who displace their anger, like the victim of spousal abuse who turns and abuses her children or the child who is teased by his peers that turns around and hurt younger children.

People who allow their anger to overtake them lose perspective and are unable to think about consequences. The intense feelings of anger are seen as the result of an activating event (in Cain's case Abel getting in the way of his offering being favored and thus becoming God's favorite) that keeps them from achieving a goal. The person's belief about the event is the fuel that intensifies their anger; Abel did not get in the way of Cain being God's favorite; Cain's heart got in the way because he allowed anger to take up residence there.

Anger affects us physically, emotionally, and spiritually

How much more grievous are the consequences of anger than the causes of it.

-**Marcus Aurelius**

Approximately twenty percent of the general population has levels of hostility that are high enough to be dangerous to their health. Because of unresolved anger, many people suffer in their bodies, mind, and spirit. A number of physical and mental illnesses are linked to stress caused by chronic anger. This stress reaction manifests as psychosomatic conditions, like chronic headache, backache, and other illnesses. The negative effects of anger were not part of God's original plan for us.

The word of God says that we are fearfully and wonderfully made and that his thoughts towards us are for good and not evil, to give us a future and a hope. His original plan for mankind was to live forever with him in an environment that supplied their every need, a place of tranquility without the worry of physical or psychological threat. The fall of mankind forced us to live in a world filled with real and perceived danger (natural and man-made disasters). Cain said to God, "Surely you have driven me out this day from the face of the ground; I shall be hidden from your face; I shall be a fugitive and a vagabond on the earth, and it will happen that anyone who finds me will kill me."

Cain's angry response set in motion a chain of events that led to both an increase in negative consequences (fear, anxiety), and the strengthening of the internal warning system (fight or flight mechanism); this mechanism was created for your protection, to warn you about impending danger, but left unchecked causes harm to your body. The Fight or Flight response is an internal warning signal that alerts you to real and perceived threat, and thus ensures physical survival. Your body prepares itself, when confronted by a threat, such as a wild animal or an angry person that is about to attack, and gives you the choice to either stand your ground and fight or run away.

When you are faced with a person or situation that threatens you physically or psychologically, the fight or flight mechanism is activated and leads to a surge of adrenaline and other stress hormones; breathing, oxygen consumption, and vigilance increases giving you a sense of power. The activation of this mechanism accounts for sweaty palms, rapid breathing, and feeling like you have butterflies in your stomach. The downside to this response to danger is that the increase in these stress hormones causes cumulative danger to your system, including long-term negative medical outcomes like stress related illness.

According to research done by professionals in the field of anger management, anger is hazardous to your health; since it is directly related to arousal of the autonomic nervous system and the functioning of the immune system; it likely increases overall vulnerability to illness. What does this mean to you, as you deal with the daily hazards of increased exposure to anger and angry people? The more you are exposed to inappropriate and unregulated displays of anger and the more you allow anger to control you, the more vulnerable you are to disease.

The effects of anger are not only felt physically, but also take an emotional toll. It has been said that depression is anger turned inward, a result of one's inability to express and deal assertively with intense anger or simmering resentment. Anger can be internalized as a result of hidden sin (like an extramarital affair) causing shame and guilt, leaving you depressed and feeling helpless and hopeless, unable to fulfill God's purpose in your life.

The emotional toll of anger that results in depression reaches back to biblical times. Many of the people in the bible experienced sadness and depression, but none expressed it as eloquently as David in the book of Psalms. He cried out to the Lord and said, "The health was taken from my bones because of my sin." David's anger and depression weighed on him like a heavy burden that made him "bow-down, causing him to mourn all day long."

Your choices in life sometimes lead to negative outcomes and causes anger and depression. David, a man of God, made one such choice when he slept with Bathsheba, the wife of Uriah. She became pregnant by David, so he attempted to cover his sin by summoning her husband from the battlefield to lay with her. David's plan failed when Uriah did not sleep with his wife. He became angry and placed him at the forefront of the hottest battle, where he died.

When David's sin came to God's attention, He sent Nathan with a parable about two men, one rich and the other who was poor. Nathan told the story of the rich man who had many flocks and herds, but refused to take from his own flock to feed a traveler in need. Instead, he took the one lamb the poor man had. When David heard the parable he became angry, saying that the rich man should be put to death, "and he shall restore four-fold for the lamb because he did this thing and he had not pity."

The account in the book of Samuel said that Nathan's response to David was simply "you are the man." David came face to face with the consequences of his sin (God told him that his child from the liaison with Bathsheba would die, and adversity would come against him and his house) and he became angry and extremely depressed (2 Samuel 12:17). Facing the consequences of your actions, especially when they cause pain to a loved one, can cause you to internalize your anger, resulting in physical illness, emotional turmoil, and spiritual stagnation.

We know that unregulated anger triggers a stress reaction that produces hormones that can accumulate in the body and cause physical damage; research in the field of stress management looks at the correlation between increased stress hormones (like cortisol) and heart disease and even cancer. Chronic feelings of anger are also known to increase anxiety levels and depression, but how does it affect the spirit?

The book of Proverbs refers to the spirit of a man as "the lamp of the Lord, searching all the inner depths of his heart." Imagine your spirit searching each room of your heart. At the end of the search it must give a report to the Lord. What will that report say about the state of your spirit? Is anger hidden in the chambers of your heart? Unresolved anger is like a blanket that covers the spirit and dims God's light that shines through the soul and searches for areas in need of a healing touch. God's light is unable to flow through these areas, causing spiritual illness. *Remember, a man's spirit is the only part of himself that will survive the first death, and is then committed into the hands of God.*

Unresolved anger can stagnate your spiritual growth, cause spiritual atrophy, and ultimately affect your relationship with God. People who allow their anger to simmer invest time and energy ensuring that the fire of their anger does not go out. The energy diverted to this cause, is taken from two areas: 1-Your connection to God through prayer 2-Your trust in God (willingness to open up to God and receive a healing touch).

1. Your connection to God through prayer

Jesus describes Himself in the book of John as the "true vine" and His Father as the "vine-dresser". We are described as the branches, which receive nutrients from the vine in order to bear good fruit. Branches cannot maintain their existence apart from the vine, nor can they bear fruits without the nutrition they receive from it. Unresolved anger creates a blockage that stops the nutrients from getting from the vine to the branches, much like a blocked artery prevents the blood supply to major organs.

A person whose arteries are blocked require medical attention to unblock the artery and allow the free flow of blood supply to the organs; without this procedure, the blood will not flow appropriately to those areas, resulting in atrophy and death of the organ. There are several ways to repair a blocked artery: Bypass the damaged vessel to allow life-giving blood to reach the dying areas; use Angioplasty, in which a balloon-like instrument is inserted to inflate the artery and unblock it.

Anger is similar to the buildup of cholesterol and fat in the walls of your arteries; it will harden your heart and spirit, causing a spiritual blockage. The book of Hebrews warns against this by saying "Do not harden your hearts as in the rebellion, in the day of trial in the wilderness." Life circumstances and disappointments can cause you to harden your heart and separate you from the life-giving vine. This spiritual separation from the vine deprives you of the most basic nutrients that are life sustaining.

You don't have to go very far for examples of spiritual blockage; think about that friend or relative who remains adamant about not going to church, not believing in God, or getting involved with those "hypocritical Christians" in church. At the core you might uncover unresolved anger caused by hurt and pain inflicted by a thoughtless individual. The loss of a loved one can also cause some to become angry and harden their hearts. The friend who lost a son in a fire and lost his faith in God, the cousin who left church because of backstabbing members, or the stranger who does not trust God because his prayers were not answered, all have one thing in common: the accumulation of pain, like plaque, hardened their hearts and blocked God's love from penetrating.

Sometimes, God has to perform a spiritual Angioplasty to clean out the blocked vessels in your heart and allow the free flow of his spirit in your life. God can only diagnose the condition if you maintain the connection, allowing him to look at those areas that are hurting. Following God's assessment, diagnosis, and surgical intervention, you may end up out of commission for a few days; use this time of rest and recuperation from spiritual surgery to think about the types of spiritual food you feed your heart and how they contributed to your current condition. Ask yourself the following questions: Am I feasting on anger? Am I harboring unforgiveness? Am I allowing jealousy to rule in my heart? Is my diet devoid of God's word? Am I spending time with Him, will I allow him to heal me?

2. Your trust in God (willingness to open up to God and receive a healing touch)

When you allow your anger to separate you from the "true vine" you cut out the only source of spiritual nutrition and deny you the healing touch for which Jesus was beaten and crucified (Isaiah 53:5...and by His stripes we are healed). Allowing your anger to become an obstacle that blocks His spirit from flowing through those dark areas in your life in need of healing is like rejecting the procedure that will unblock the vessels to your heart.

Jesus is described as the great physician who came to Earth to heal those who are physically, emotionally, and spiritually sick. Anger may not be considered a physical or emotional illness but can cause you to become emotionally paralyzed; it stops you from going forward in your life, instead it renders you helpless like the paralyzed man in the book of Matthew, whose friends lowered him down from the ceiling to be healed. Jesus said to the paralyzed man, "son, be of good cheer; your sins are forgiven you....Arise, take up your bed, and go to your house." Likewise I say to you don't allow anger to cause a spiritual paralysis that keeps you from walking in God's promises. Get up! Lay down your anger, pick up forgiveness, and get on with your life.

Tom is a 56-year-old man who allowed his anger to paralyze him like the man in the book of Matthew. He allowed an indiscretion twenty-five-years earlier between his wife and best friend to ruin his friendship and threaten the success of his business. Tom was a successful businessman who dedicated his life to building a consulting firm with his college buddy. He recalls the days he and Bill (his business partner and friend) sat around the dorms dreaming of making it big in the business world; he also recalls wanting to get married to his High School sweetheart, and have children. Those were the simple days he said! "We said we would conquer the world with our youth and idealism, and we did."

After 25 years of friendship and fifteen years of having a successful business partnership, Tom found out that Bill and Susan (Tom's wife) had a very brief affair while in college. The relationship was short lived; in fact, it ended after two dates. Bill, a new convert to Christ was unable to live with the secret knowledge of his affair with Susan (Tom's girlfriend at the time); he struggled with the thought of hurting his friend, but could not endure hiding the truth any longer; following a dinner party, Bill disclosed the affair to Tom who responded angrily, ending the friendship.

Bill anticipated Tom's anger, but expected to be forgiven following a cooling off period; the reality however, was much different. Tom refused to hear any excuses from his friend and threatened to dissolve the business along with the friendship, but relented about the business after thinking things over. Tom allowed his hurt feelings, however, to erect a wall of anger and unforgiveness that ended his long-term friendship with Bill. His unforgiveness surprised everyone, especially Bill; after all, Tom led him to Christ earlier that year and taught him about the need to forgive. Bill recalls thinking that if anyone would be quick to forgive; it would be Tom, to Bill's surprise that did not happen.

Two years later Bill and Tom are still at odds; Tom refuses to talk to Bill, even though they continue to be business partners. Tom believes that he can never trust his former friend again. His unforgiveness not only cost him his friendship with Bill, it also threatened the continued success of the business, and the closeness he enjoyed in his relationship with Christ. Tom's prayer life suffered, causing a spiritual disconnect; he became so angry he stopped praying, blaming God for allowing the affair to happen; his ability to manage the company was greatly hindered, because of the lack of communication with his business partner (Bill was his sounding board and the person he brainstormed with about important business decisions). The lack of cooperation became evident in the loss of revenue and customer base. Tom allowed his anger to emotionally paralyze him; stopping him from moving on in his friendship with Bill and successfully going forward with the company they built.

Tom's anger became a cancer that slowly infected his friendship and business partnership with Bill; most importantly it hindered his prayer life, reducing communication with the source of healing, Jesus! His anger almost severed his connection to the true vine, leaving him vulnerable and paralyzed in the face of the problem. Anger is infectious! It infects your relationship with people close to you. Like an infection that spreads from organ to organ, your anger will spread from one relationship to the other; eventually it will affect your relationship with God.

Displacing your anger creates a chasm that makes you feel like God has moved away; this divide or separation can diminish your trust in God's ability to change your situation and cause you to feel stuck or paralyzed. Tom created a wall with his anger that soon blocked God's healing from penetrating.

Have you allowed your anger to sever your connection to the vine? Take a time out to reconnect to Jesus, the great physician! During his walk through this Earth, many came to be healed from their suffering; people came from far away and overcame great obstacles just to benefit from Jesus' healing touch. Forsaking all, they came tearing down walls that previously separated them from Christ. They came open and willing to do whatever it took to be healed; some allowed Jesus to place a mudpack full of saliva on their eyes to regain their eyesight. What will it take for you to regain your eyesight/insight? Are you willing to forsake anger to receive a touch from Jesus in your life? Answer the following questions prior to completing the journal on the next page.

1. Am I willing to lose anger to gain healing?
2. On a scale from 1 to 10, how much value do I place on my anger?
3. Who am I really angry with?
4. What does it mean to give my anger over to God?
5. If I gave up my anger, what will I be left with?

Complete the following prayer journal

Dear Lord, my diet has been devoid of the spiritual nutrients I need for a healthy spiritual heart and I've allowed my anger to be the junk food I feasted on; please _____

_____

_____

_____

The tentacles of unresolved anger are indeed far reaching; they invade all three areas of your life ensuring a slow spiritual death and illness in the body and mind. There is a form of anger that is even more insidious; one you think is no longer there but lurks in the dark places of your mind buried in your unconscious pretending to no longer affect you, but it does. This type of anger is sometimes unrecognized and may manifest in disguise as feelings of irritability towards a specific person or current situation.

Repressed anger

Buried anger is never dead, it will resurrect if not dealt with. People repress emotions that are unacceptable, like putting a lid on the coffin of your anger, hoping it will never come to light. You may deny being angry because you have feelings of guilt, shame, or fear. These feelings are often outside your awareness and may manifest as frustration, disappointment, or vague feelings of being let down. It is difficult to pinpoint how you are feeling or why you are feeling that way, making it easy to displace your anger on something or someone else.

Unconscious, repressed, anger surfaces at the most inopportune times, like when you are dealing with people and situations that are not connected with the cause of your anger. For example, a person (we will refer to as Robert) flies off the handle and argues with a total stranger when she voices her opinion about lazy people. The unsuspecting stranger is unaware that the phrase she used contained a trigger word or a stepped on land mine in Robert's head.

Looking back at Robert's life shows a picture of a self-proclaimed, laid back individual who does not base his schedule on other people's schedule; he is perceived as not being pro-active, taking his time to get things done. Growing up, he was told that he was lazy and would not amount to anything in a world that values people with energy and drive.

Robert believes that people should chill instead of running around like chickens with their heads cut off.

His early experiences in life were painted with a brush of hostility towards him and others who are laid back. He learned that the words *laid back* were synonymous with lazy and therefore had a negative connotation. Even though he never attempted to change his behavior, Robert harbored anger and resentment toward the people in his past that perceived him as lazy. Anytime Robert heard the word lazy, it registered on his internal thermometer, causing a rise in temperature.

Because Robert was unable to deal with these unacceptable feelings of anger towards the people in his past, he suppressed them (a conscious process). As these feelings tried to resurface, they were further buried in the unconscious through a process called repression (the mind stores the memories out of immediate consciousness). Often, these repressed emotions are accessed during harmless situations that trigger a reaction and cause the individual to *displace* their anger.

Some people go through an entire lifetime carrying the coffin containing their repressed anger. We can all relate to a situation early in life that caused us pain and left us feeling helpless and hopeless. The underlying pain caused by the situation, becomes too much to handle, causing you to protect the resulting (emotional) wound by growing a scab-like shield (most often anger) that hides the pain.

Like a wound that needs to be left uncovered to prevent moisture buildup and allow the healing process to take place, so is your anger in need of open communication and forgiveness to prevent the buildup of resentment and allow healing. Repressed anger is like a scab that covers underlying emotions, kept below the surface in the dark areas of the mind. They say confession is good for the soul! Talking about your feelings with the person who hurt you may lead to clarification and problem resolution. If you are unable or unwilling to talk to the person who hurt you, talk to your pastor or a counselor to seek guidance about handling the situation appropriately. Avoiding the problem is never an option; it will resurface if you ignore it.

The inability or unwillingness to express your anger is due to mistaken beliefs you hold about it. Some people believe the following myths about anger: Nice people don't get angry, anger is bad, other people make you angry, you should not show your anger, you have no control over your anger, and anger hurts people. Where do people get these beliefs about anger? They are taught in your family of origin (the acceptable way of dealing with anger in the family), through environmental influence (neighborhood violence, school shootings, friends, violence on television); these beliefs are reinforced by genetic predisposition such as temperament and personality (the way you perceive and deal with situations).

Earlier in this chapter, I said that anger is not bad, it is a normal emotion placed in you by God. Your anger can energize and motivate you to take action in a situation that is unfair, it can cause you to do something about an injustice, or it can even motivate you to write a book. Anger becomes a problem when it is used to cover other emotions, when it becomes an excuse for your behavior, when it is repressed, and when you allow it to control others or you.

Why do you allow your anger to get out of control when you know the outcome will be negative? The answer to this question may be found in the answer to these questions: Why do we overeat? Why do we choose to ignore God's will in our lives? Why do we spend too much? Why do we hang on to angry feelings? I believe the answer lies in the immediate gratification or payoff we receive. We know that being overweight is the cost of overeating and the wages of sin is death, we also know that overspending can lead to financial ruin and that hanging on to anger causes negative outcomes, but the immediate and short-term payoff (feeling good temporarily, and immediate gratification) often outweighs the long-term cost.

The cost and payoff of your anger:

Unregulated and uncontrolled anger comes with a high price tag. The person who allows his/her anger to cloud their judgment uses hurtful words or actions to get their point across. The teenager who does not get what she wants and says, "I hate you Mom and Dad," the wife who feels hurt and gives her husband the silent treatment, all allowed their anger to dictate their behavior. The result of these and other negative interactions strain relationships, cause shame and guilt, and erode communication.

Who thinks about consequences when it feels so good to give someone a piece of your mind? After all, that person really made you mad. All behavior is goal directed, even when the behavior seems crazy. The teenager who screams at her parents is trying to individuate, flex her muscles, and gain power; the wife who gives her husband the silent treatment is saying you hurt me and the only way I can hurt you back is not to allow you back in my world, at least temporarily. In all of these scenarios, the goal of their anger is to gain power. This behavior often comes at a hefty cost to the relationship, erodes trust, and blocks effective communication.

As you evaluate the cost of your unregulated anger, you may think to yourself, maybe I should have refrained from saying those nasty things to my loved one or my parents; if only I could have predicted the consequences of my angry words, I would have chosen my words more carefully or taken a different course of action. The reality is that sometimes people do what feels good at the time, even if they are able to predict the outcome.

Review the following list of physical, behavioral, psychological, and spiritual cost of uncontrolled anger:

- Loss of health
- Muscle tension
- Increased stress
- Tension headaches

- Losing your temper
- Spousal abuse
- Child abuse
- Depression
- Anxiety
- A general sense of unhappiness
- Cognitive distortions/irrational thinking
- Losing your family
- Losing friendships
- Loss of freedom because of a prison sentence
- Spiritual numbness/apathy
- Loss of connection with God

Anger is a normal and automatic reaction to real or perceived injustice. Allowing it to spin out-of-control and hurt others or yourself is not normal. What has your anger cost you recently?

Complete the following sentences, and list the physical, emotional, relational and spiritual cost of your anger in each case:

1. When someone ignores me I _____
   _____
   _____

2. When someone does something that makes me feel sad I _____
   _____
   _____

3. When I get angry I _____
   _____
   _____

4. When I'm angry for a period of time, my spiritual life becomes _____
   _____
   _____

5. When I become angry with my spouse or loved one I _____
   _____

6.   Arguing my point makes me feel _____

_____

_____

7.   Physically, my anger has cost me _____

_____

_____

8.   Emotionally, my anger has cost me _____

_____

_____

9.   Spiritually, my anger has cost me _____

_____

_____

10. My anger cost me the following relationships _____

_____

_____

The above sentence completion exercise allows you to explore your immediate and most honest thoughts about your anger. Take a moment to review the cost, if any, of your unregulated anger and write a journal.

_____

_____

_____

Some people are willing to pay the cost for their unregulated and out-of-control anger in order to enjoy a very temporary sense of satisfaction. You don't have to look too far for examples. Think about the person who knows he is wrong for screaming and hanging up on the poor telemarketer on the phone, but says "it felt so good." The rush he gets from taking his frustrations out on the unsuspecting person who is doing his job gives a sense of immediate satisfaction. The payoff for your angry outburst outweighs the delayed consequences, making it easier to choose what feels good right now.

Payoffs are the rewards or good feeling you get in response to an angry outburst; for example, you may feel energized by the surge of adrenaline that comes from the sense of readiness to fight the person or run away from the situation. The release of anger can also give a sense of temporary satisfaction and a vague notion that the matter is resolved (at least in your head). Anger also gives an illusion of power. The book of Proverbs puts it this way: "The wrath of a king is like the roaring of a lion." A lion is a very powerful animal; his power comes from his strength and the loud roar that keeps others away. The powerful roar of *your* anger acts like a shield that keeps people at a distance.

Behaviors are not repeated unless they are reinforced. As stated earlier in the chapter, all behavior is goal-directed and is positively or negatively reinforced. The lion's roar is enough to reinforce fear in other animals and humans. The lion learned that he does not have to attack to instill fear and keep other animals away after watching their reaction to his roar. Your anger is also sufficient to reinforce fear in others and serve as a protective shield.

How are behaviors reinforced? Behaviors are reinforced by the attention they garner anytime they happen. For example, a child who receives little or no attention from his parents may try to bring the spotlight on himself by misbehaving. If the parents consistently respond by yelling at the child, their attention, although negative, will reinforce his bad behavior. A teenager seeking attention from her father may yell at the top of her lungs and angrily destroy her room to get him to intervene. She has been unsuccessful in the past when she tries to talk to him calmly about her feelings because he blows her off with a quick "let's talk later." She soon learns that her violent outburst is the only way of getting immediate attention.

Payoffs result from the positive or negative reinforcement you receive for your behavior. You've heard the saying "negative attention is better than no attention." The basic idea is to get attention by whatever means necessary, thus fulfilling a goal. Anger sometimes becomes the shield that protects people from hurt and pain, or the tonic that gives them a sense of strength against a perpetrator (the goal is protection from pain or to gain strength against a perpetrator). This angry behavior is reinforced when you feel protected from those who can inflict pain on you because you are able to keep them at a safe distance.

When there is a consistent payoff for your anger, you are more likely to repeat the angry behavior that produced the reward, thus reinforcing it. A gang member, for example, may get rewarded for his violent behavior from several places: attention from the media, the respect of fellow gang members, and the fear he instills in the public. The intangible payoff for his violent behavior gives him a sense of power and control that he will likely not want to relinquish.

The following is a list of payoffs that reinforce your anger:

- Not wanting to forgive because you feel justified in your anger
- Exerting control over other people with your angry behavior
- Having the satisfaction of saying, "I'm right"
- Being a victim and making the other person feel sorry for you
- Manipulating others with your anger
- Not taking responsibility for your behavior
- Blaming others for your reaction
- Keeping others at a distance with your anger
- Protecting your self-esteem with your anger

- Hiding your fear
- Not opening yourself to love, keeping it safe

What is or has been the payoff for your anger? Complete the following sentences honestly to determine what reinforces your anger.

1. I feel a sense of _____
   _____, when I win an argument.
2. Being right means _____
   _____
   _____
3. I use my anger to _____
   _____
   _____
4. I define anger as _____
   _____
   _____
5. When I get angry, others react to me by _____
   _____
   _____

Perhaps you don't use your anger to control or protect yourself from others, but your anger has been controlling you. If your anger has taken on a life of its own, it may be time to explore the purpose it serves in your life. Is your anger the lid that covers and keeps other emotions from surfacing? Dealing with feelings of sadness or anxiety can prove to be emotionally more difficult than expressing feelings of anger.

Chapter 2

ANGER IS A SECONDARY EMOTION

What is underneath your anger?

Human beings are resilient and fragile at the same time, like a spider web, delicate and strong. We are able to survive the most unspeakable tragedies (an earthquake or hurricane) but at times, we fall apart when we feel rejected or afraid. The bible speaks to the fragility of man/woman, comparing us to a flower that appears one day and disappears the next. Our timeframe on Earth is short and full of emotional ups and downs, but we are able to summon defenses that guard us against great pain. These defenses aren't always positive, but are useful in the short-run, providing a temporary shield that gives us a sense of emotional safety.

Anger can be one of those defenses you use as a shield to protect you from dealing with deeper, underlying emotions. These primary emotions, such as fear, are suppressed and kept from immediate access by a secondary and more powerful emotion called anger. Have you ever noticed people who wear a frown on their face, always appearing to be angry at the world? Maybe you are that person who wears the frown and others go out of their way to avoid you. Your shield of anger protects you, while keeping others at bay. These underlying feelings like fear, sadness, and low self-worth, make you feel vulnerable and in need of protection from others.

In the previous chapter, I used the analogy of the scab covering a wound that needs oxygen to heal to explain how anger sometimes covers other emotions and bury pain that needs to be exposed and dealt with in order to heal. If you were to take off the scab of anger, what emotions would bubble to the surface? Peeling back your anger may put you in touch with an array of emotions you have covered over the years, such as feelings of sadness that stems from years of physical, verbal, or sexual abuse. Maybe your anger does not cover feelings resulting from trauma; however, it can hide loneliness or feelings of inadequacy. Although unregulated anger is not always used to keep you from dealing with underlying emotions, it can keep them from being uncovered. Review the following list of emotions and ask yourself which one of these you are covering with anger?

- Anxiety
- Fear
- Frustration
- Sadness
- Disappointment
- Hopelessness and Helplessness
- Low self-esteem
- Feelings of inadequacy
- Shame
- Guilt

Your anger may or may not conceal deep feelings you are not willing to deal with. If you do not use your anger to conceal other emotions, you are part of a small group of people who have learned to face their emotions head on. Don't panic if you belong to the larger group who hides painful feelings with their anger. Maybe you were raised in a family that found value in stuffing feelings and keeping silent to protect yourself and others, a family whose expressions of emotions, like fear and sadness, are taboo. Perhaps you are not quite sure how to express your feelings, keeping a lid on them until they become too overwhelming to contain. No matter what the reason for concealing your emotions, it always builds up and spills over when you least expect it. Uncovering what's underneath your anger may be the first step in managing it.

Complete the following exercise by connecting your anger to one or more of the primary feelings to the right. Fill in the blank spaces provided, with additional emotions.

Anger   Sadness
                                         Fear
                                         Loneliness
                                         Depression
                                         Shame

                                         _____
                                         _____
                                         _____

Why is it safer to show anger in lieu of other emotions? This is not an easy question to answer. The way a person expresses emotions is based on a number of variables like personality/temperament, genetics, culture, gender, and environmental/societal cues. These variables determine what feelings are safe, when they are safe to express, how to express them, and if they are safe to express. For example, the open expression of sadness is more acceptable from females than from males, in most cultures. If a man openly cries in public he may be perceived as weak and vulnerable (although this is slowly changing) but if he expresses that sadness through his anger he feels safer and not at risk of being judged a softy.

The fear of becoming vulnerable around others coupled with temperament or cultural predisposition makes it difficult for some people to express emotions like sadness, or fear of abandonment over their anger. The answer to the above question might be: *It is more acceptable to be considered a lion, keeping people at bay with your roar of anger, than to be a chicken, something others can have for lunch.* Regardless of your reason for using anger to cover other emotions, one thing is certain: Issues brought on by the underlying feeling will go unresolved!

The energy required to keep your emotions in check is enormous and takes a physical, emotional, and spiritual toll on you. Anger, like the lid on the pressure cooker, keeps other emotions from surfacing and places you at risk of a blowout. This secondary emotion covers raw feelings that would otherwise emerge and uncover deep pain. The list of emotions concealed by your anger can be extensive, however, one particular emotion seems to be the common denominator for most people's anger: fear!

What's fear got to do with it?

Some dictionaries define fear as an anxiety caused by real or possible danger. It is also defined as an awe or reverence for something, as in "the fear of the Lord is the beginning of wisdom." The word fear took on a new meaning on September 11, 2001, and in the months following the terrorist attacks. Americans and people around the world experienced tremendous levels of anxiety, not knowing if another terrorist attack might occur. A thick scab of anger, that would emotionally keep many from ever feeling vulnerable again, soon covered the fear that gripped the world during that period. Many used this protective shield as a war banner that announced, "I cannot be victimized."

The problem with covering or trying to suppress one's emotions is they soon find their way to the surface. As those competing emotions try to resurface, putting you in contact with your limitations, they produce more frustration and anger. This vicious cycle only produces more violent behavior, less patience, and an overall decrease in people's ability to cope with stress. Is there a connection between fear and violence? The answer to this question is beyond the scope of this book; however, following 9/11, many people reported feeling more fear and anger.

Fear is normal and a very human emotion! Unfortunately, it is also synonymous with vulnerability and a sense of helplessness and hopelessness. You may erroneously conclude that to feel fear is to be weak and to be angry is to show strength. These conclusions perpetuate the need to rely on anger to deal with more vulnerable feelings that are a normal part of life. The expression of fear is not new; it was first documented in the book of Genesis when God took His blessing from Cain after he killed his brother Abel. God cursed Cain and told him that he would roam the Earth as an unprotected vagabond, at the mercy of anyone who found him. Cain responded with fear. He told God that the punishment was too great to bear.

As paralyzing as fear can be, there is an antidote. The bible tells us that with every trying circumstance, God has made a way to deal with it. *Perfect love cast out fear!* The word, perfect love in the scripture refers to a mature love; it also refers to the type of love that encompasses everything you need to succeed in life. This Agape love is found in Christ, who takes care of every worry or anxiety you may have. Before you choose to cover your fear using the shield of anger for protection, consider putting on the shield of God's righteousness that protects you from every fiery dart that comes from the enemy.

Complete the following prayer journal

Dear Lord my fear has ——————————————————

_____

_____

_____

_____

_____

_____

_____

_____

_____

_____

_____

_____

_____

_____

_____

_____

_____

_____

_____

_____

_____

_____

_____

_____

_____

_____

_____

_____

_____

_____

_____

_____

We want what we want, when we want it

Everything that is in agreement with our personal desires seems true. Everything that is not puts us in a rage
-Andre Maurois

People are born pleasure seeking and egocentric, concerned only with self-gratification. A newborn's main goal is to satisfy his needs when wet, hungry, cold, or hot, he becomes upset and cries and Mom takes care of his needs. As you grow, you learn to delay self-gratification in order to be accepted in society. Imagine after being potty trained, years later you decided to forgo using the toilette and wet your pants instead to prove a point; perhaps you felt the urge to scream *fire* in the middle of a theater filled with people because it felt good! Fortunately, maturity dampens this egocentric urge to "have it my way"—or does it?

Most people mature and learn to delay self-gratification, however, there are a small percentage of time when you find yourself becoming angry when you don't get what you want. You are not alone! A number of people become highly upset when life doesn't line up with their personal desires. These are the times when you may be tempted to use God as a genie in a bottle that is released to fulfill your three wishes. When He decides not to grant your wish, what is your response? Are you a force to be reckoned with? Not getting your wants and expectations met may cause you to lose your cool, especially when you believe you deserved it.

Sometimes life circumstances don't line up with your personal desires, at times making unexpected turns. Do you escalate into a rage or spiral out-of-control when things don't turn out the way you expected them to? Do you host a pity party and invite your friends to the festivities or do you keep them away with your angry disposition? If you answered yes to these questions, you are part of the elite group of divas who wants what they want, when they want it.

Christine prayed for months that God would save her

husband, Joe, and that he would lead a different lifestyle, one that placed his family as a priority. Over the years, she communicated her disapproval of Joe's lifestyle and told him that it caused the family pain. After a few years of complaining, Christine felt that her words were falling on deaf ears and decided not to talk with Joe about his behavior, but to pray instead.

Several months later, Joe left the family to further pursue his lifestyle. He got involved with another woman who went to church regularly and she invited him to her church, where Joe accepted the Lord. Christine became angry and began blaming God for her husband's departure. She asked God why he did not save her husband while they were together, instead changing him for the benefit of someone else.

Christine wanted Joe to be saved while he was in a relationship with her, not after he was gone. She could not understand why God did not answer her prayer when she first made her request. What is the point of him being saved after he left! "I'm not benefiting from the change," she said. Christine became angry with God and stopped praying, to her detriment and that of her family. She was unwilling to see the blessing in Joe's salvation and allowed her anger to interfere in her relationship with God. Christine did not get what she wanted when she wanted it and it made her angry.

If Christine were to look back on the relationship and explore her true feelings, she may have realized that what she wanted was a change in her husband's behavior and for him to adjust to her expectations. She expected God to change Joe in order to meet her needs, not necessarily for his salvation towards eternal life.

Have you ever been hurt by someone or witnessed an injustice perpetrated by a person, only to see them prosper and receive God's blessings? You may have thought it not fair that someone who does wrong should be rewarded. How is it that people who do bad things seem to enjoy good things while others (good people), suffer loss? I want to see that person punished now! How can God allow them to get away with that? You ask yourself, all the while thinking God is falling asleep on the job. Aren't you glad that we are not in charge of deciding who deserves a blessing and whom God should punish? In your righteous indignation (the Christian word for anger), you are likely to send even a repentant person to hell.

Jonah, like many of you, believed he should have his way, even if it meant God punishing an entire city. When God called Jonah to preach to the people in Nineveh regarding their sins, he fled in the opposite direction. Jonah later confided that he knew God would relent and forgive the people, and therefore, he chose not to go. His attempt to escape his responsibilities was short lived, landing him instead in a very precarious situation. Jonah's heart was not set to please God, but to please him based on his understanding of the way things should work.

God saved Jonah from his hardened heart by allowing a big fish to swallow him. He sent him to Nineveh to preach His word so that the people might be saved. When you listen to this story, you may have, in the past, focused on Jonah's disobedience and God's mercy on him. Jonah's angry response towards God, after he preached and the people of Nineveh's repentance is seldom the focus. The fourth chapter of the book of Jonah tells us that he became angry because God relented after the people came to repentance, and God did not destroy the city. Jonah did not get what he wanted (to see the people of Nineveh punished for their deeds) and became angry. He could not understand why God would save a city of people who were wicked, so he asked God to take his life.

Perhaps you would never go to the extreme of asking God to take your life because things did not work out the way you wanted. You may even think, how silly of Jonah to want to die because things did not go his way. Sometimes, you can allow your anger to take control of you and cause a level of emotional pain that increases your vulnerability for suicide.

Points for discussion

Anger is considered a secondary emotion; it is not the first emotion we experience, but often the first one we recognize. Cultural and gender differences influences the way we deal with emotions and sometimes dictate whether we should openly deal with or conceal our feelings

1. What emotion do you have trouble expressing?
2. What does the bible say about fear?
3. Are you currently dealing with sadness?
4. Do you mask sadness with anger?
5. Who created your emotions?
6. Can you tell the difference between when you are sad and angry?
7. What lessons did you learn about anger, in your family of origin?
8. What have you done with past hurts?
9. Have you begun the process of forgiveness?
10. Have you forgiven yourself?

During this segment, explore your wants and desires versus your needs. The bible tells us that God is your provider and he will meet all your needs; sometimes you may confuse a need with a want. This confusion may cause you to become angry with God, when you perceive that He is not meeting your needs.

1. Do you need a car or a Mercedes Benz?
2. Do you need a place to live or a five-bedroom house on the beach?
3. When your spouse chooses not to go with you to the opera, is he/she ignoring your needs?
4. What is the difference between a need and a want?
5. Can you meet everyone's needs?
6. Can they meet all of your needs?

Chapter 3

CHOOSING TO BE A THERMOSTAT

The way a man thinks about himself is what he becomes

-Proverbs 23:7

This chapter is based on the premise that you have the ability to choose between good or bad and right or wrong. You can also choose to allow your anger to escalate into negative behaviors or positively re-direct it in order to resolve a problem. Your anger cannot change people; neither can it change your circumstances. You are able, however, to change the negative and destructive effects of your anger by regulating it.

From the beginning, man had the ability to choose between good and evil. When God told Adam and Eve that they should not eat the fruit from the tree of knowledge of good and evil, He did not take away their ability to make that choice. God told Adam that if he ate from the tree of knowledge of good and evil, "he would surely die," which acknowledges consequences for making the wrong choice. If, therefore, there was a consequence, implicitly there was also a choice.

The choices people make are often affected by their assumptions; similarly the choice to react or act in a given situation is also affected by assumptions about the situation, and the people involved. Based on the biblical principal that a person becomes what he believes *"as a man thinks so is he"* and Albert Ellis' Rational Emotive Behavior Therapy, this chapter demonstrates that your belief system determine your circumstances, not the events in your life. It also raises the argument that you can choose to regulate your anger and therefore modify the outcome, or you can angrily react to your circumstances and have the outcome regulate you.

Thermostat vs. Thermometer

Verbalizing the mechanical differences between a thermometer and a thermostat is relatively easy. Most people can determine their use and tell you their approximate location in the home or in a building. The functional differences of these instruments, however, confuses some, leaving them at a lost for words when asked how they affect the environment or are affected by it. Some people believe both instruments are only affected by the environment and do not have the capability to change the climate by acting on it. Similarly, they believe that their anger is solely affected by external factors such as other people and situations, and therefore they have no control over it.

What is the difference between these instruments? A thermometer is an instrument that is used for measuring the temperature; the mercury rises and falls as it adjusts to external conditions to indicate change. A thermostat is an apparatus that regulates the temperature, changing room temperature from hot to cold or vice versa. The thermostat affects the environment, while the thermometer is affected by it.

Much like these two instruments, you can allow your anger to be affected by the environment or you can regulate your anger in spite of the environment. Although bad things happen in life, you have a choice in your responses. For example, Jim (who often thinks of himself as a victim) was having a bad day following a delay he experienced standing in line at the bank. The teller, a white male, closed his window as Jim approached it. He reacted with rage and began arguing with the teller and others around him, stating that the teller closed the window because of the color of his skin. Using a model that shows Activating event or situation, Belief system, and Consequences, let's explore Jim's behavior:

A- **Activating event**: Teller closed the window as Jim approached.

B- **Belief process**: Jim's cognition or thought process about himself and the event, "I'm a victim and others will try to victimize me. The teller closed the window because of the color of my skin."

C- **Consequence**: Jim's rage and argumentative behavior towards the teller and others.

The activating event did not cause Jim's rage. His assumptions or beliefs about the teller being prejudice fueled Jim's anger and caused him to become enraged. In the same manner, a person who reacts like a thermometer allows their assumptions or beliefs to be the mercury that gauges the intent of others rather than making an objective appraisal about the situation.

1. The thermometer: The situation determines your behavior

Some people wear their emotions on their sleeves. Something happens that affects them or affects their surroundings and it immediately elicits a reaction. They show their feelings about the event before it even registers in their brain. The thermometer may say things like, "I can't help my reactions or the way I feel," or "He made me mad," or "Anytime I see that person my skin crawls." You are generally driven by external variables, like people and situations. Most of the time you react to events or situations without stopping to think about them. Something happens that changes the emotional climate and your internal mercury rises or falls.

Although you are a caring individual who is often referred to as very emotional or extremely sensitive, your cognitive appraisals about yourself and others are often negative. You constantly tell yourself that people don't like you, you are not worthy, and others only want something from you. You invest time and energy reacting to people's expressions, their words, their body language, and even another person's thoughts. At times you may even react to what you think the other person is thinking, leaving you emotionally drained by the end of the day.

Feeling helpless and hopeless you may use passive-aggressive or aggressive techniques to get your point across or you blow up inappropriately to release the buildup of emotions. You may complain to family and friends that you don't feel heard or understood, but seldom speak up for yourself. Can you identify yourself or someone you know in the following vignette?

Vignette

Susan is a 34-year-old administrative assistance who has been with the company for 5 years. She loves her job, but it can be very stressful and demanding. Her boss requires attention to detail and believes that his employees should stay until the work is done correctly. Susan wants to do an excellent job, but she is torn between the office and her husband and three small children who require her attention as well. She needs the job to supplement her husband's income and believes that it will be difficult to get another job with good benefits. Susan is frustrated and feels like a volcano inside of her is about to erupt.

Which of the following indicates that Susan's reaction is that of a thermometer? Put a check beside each statement you think makes her a thermometer.

1. Susan pulls her boss aside and talks to him about the dilemma she is having and asks for his input.
2. She talks to her husband about the stress she is experiencing and asks for his input.
3. She starts to cry and breaks down the next time her boss asks her to stay past 4:30.
4. Susan talks to one of her friends about her stress and begins to sob while she tells the story.
5. She lashes out at a customer on the phone immediately after her boss makes another unreasonable request.
6. Susan pretends she does not hear her boss' request for her to stay late and sneaks out the office leaving a very important task unfinished.
7. She badmouths her boss anytime she gets a chance.

8. Susan prays about the situation for guidance and calls her boss into a conference to talk about her options.
9. The next time her boss asks her to do something she blows up at him.
10. She does nothing.

After reading the above vignette and placing a check by each statement you feel represents a person who acts like a thermometer, complete the following journal.

Dear Lord, my anger has: _____

_____

_____

_____

_____

_____

_____

_____

_____

_____

_____

_____

_____

_____

_____

_____

_____

_____

_____

_____

_____

_____

_____

_____

_____

2. The thermostat: You regulate the outcome of your circumstance

This is the person who chooses to act rather than react to people or situations. The thermostat takes the role of the lead actor in his life, under God's direction, and uses God's word as his script. Thermostats live by and understand the scripture that tells them "As a man thinks so is he." In other words, they understand that their lives will follow their thoughts. They think about and accept situations as dynamic, always changing. This is directly opposite to the thinking of the thermometer, the person who sees situations as static and becomes despondent thinking that nothing will ever change.

A person who acts like a thermostat sets the emotional and behavioral tone in the relationship. If things are too hot he/she cools it down and conversely heats things up if they get too cold. This is the individual who refuses to go for a ride on another person's emotional roller coaster. He/she is caring, but able to set appropriate boundaries to delineate and separate his/her stuff from other people's stuff. This person is able to take responsibility for his/her feelings, actions, and behaviors, while allowing others to take responsibility for theirs.

If you are a thermostat, your boundaries are clear but flexible. You understand that you will not agree with everyone and others will not always agree with you. You accept imperfections in others and in yourself; you know that you are still a work in progress and it increases the amount of grace and mercy you show others. When your boundaries become blurred, you quickly ask for guidance (*Blessed is he who delight in God's word, and in it he meditates day and night*).

Are you a thermostat? You may find yourself moving back and forth between reacting to your circumstances with unregulated anger and responding appropriately. Cycling back and forth between these two ways of dealing with emotions does not mean that you have failed; it means you are trying to find your way. What are the characteristics that tell you someone maybe a thermostat?

Complete the following exercise by recording an event that made you angry, then record your thoughts about the event and the people involved, and finally write down any emotional, physical, or spiritual consequences:

Activating event (What happened that made you mad).

_____

_____

Your Belief (What did you think about the situation or person involved? Record any thinking errors). _____

_____

_____

Consequences; emotional, behavioral, or spiritual (What did your angry behavior cost you?) _____

_____

_____

_____

_____

_____

Chapter 4

REGULATING YOUR ANGER

Pursue peace with all men, and holiness, without which no one will see the Lord

-Hebrews 12:14

Regulating your anger will require you to **ACT-UP**: *Acknowledge* that you are angry and explore buried feelings (primary emotions) at the core of your anger. *Confess* that your anger has taken control over you, and you are willing to be accountable for it. *Trust that* God can help you regulate your anger, He gives you power over it. The final two steps in the process are crucial, but maybe more difficult. *Uproot* any bitterness and *Pray* that you do not fall into temptation to use anger as a shield.

Many people acknowledge their anger and are willing to talk to God or someone else about it, but find it difficult to take the final two steps that lead to true forgiveness. This is often difficult because it requires you to give up something, bitterness! You would assume that uprooting and giving up bitterness is an easy process. After all, it is one less piece of baggage to carry on your journey. Unfortunately, this is not true for many. You say that you want to shed excess baggage from your life, but at the end of the day you hold on to it.

The next time you are in line at the airport, watch the reaction of people when told that they are over their baggage limit. They would rather pay the cash than send the extra items home with someone. The same holds true for anger. Some people find it easier to lug it around than to give it up to God. Total surrender of your anger can be scary. It implies that you must release the other person from the debt owed to you. You may also allow the root of anger to remain in your heart because it reinforces the idea that the other person is bad and you need to protect yourself from them.

It is easy to convince yourself that you have forgiven someone. You deny that you are still angry, instead allowing those feelings to go below the surface almost undetected. Just as you think you've overcome your anger, it springs up again and again when faced with a similar situation. As a weekend gardener, I've been frustrated by the weeds that appear in my garden. I planted beautiful flowers and exotic plants, but to my surprise unwelcome weeds pop up again and again when I'm not looking. You are probably wondering what my garden has to do with regulating anger.

As I watch unwanted weeds grow in and threaten to choke out the beautiful flowers in the garden, I'm able to visualize how unregulated anger pop up in your mind and chokes out other, more appropriate, emotions. Like you, I felt totally helplessness, thinking that I had no control over the weed in my garden. Interestingly, my first line of thinking was not—get rid of them; instead I allowed myself to be overwhelmed by the weeds. I consider myself to be very assertive, decisive and able to command a following in other areas of my life, yet defeated by the weeds in my garden.

You may be a leader in other areas of your life, but find it difficult to take control of the weeds of anger. They pop up at times when you least expect them, leaving you feeling helpless and hopeless; your anger may prevent other emotions from surfacing, for example, the expression of sadness because of feelings of abandonment, you get in a rage and hurt yourself or someone else. This out-of-control anger catches you by surprise and leaves you wondering, how did I get here? Like the weeds in my garden, your anger will continue to come up until you acknowledge its presence and do something about it.

Are you a thermometer? If so, you may acknowledge your

anger, but fail to do something about it. You stand by helplessly as it takes control of your life. This is reminiscent of the gardener who does nothing to stop the weeds from taking over his garden. Your unregulated anger appears quickly and takes control, as if by surprise. Your sense of hopelessness comes from believing that nothing will ever change and you will never regain control.

Your thoughts are: *Before I knew it, the words came flying out of my mouth*, or *I can't control my temper*. This line of thinking gives way to the permissive use of uncontrolled anger to solve problems; it also implies that you have no control over your anger, moreover, others control you. In Robert's case (Chapter 1), his un-acknowledged anger popped up and ambushed the unsuspecting clerk like a dandelion in the middle of your freshly mowed lawn. Robert failed to acknowledge and deal with his anger, leading to an embarrassing situation years later. Good news! You do have control over your anger. You can be a thermostat and regulate it.

Remember, in order to regulate your anger you must:

- Acknowledge it (Psalm 32:5)

- Confess it (James5: 16; Psalm 32:5)

- Trust God (Psalm 37)

- Uproot bitterness (Hebrews 12:15; Acts 8:23)

- Pray (Phil 4:6)

Acknowledge your anger:

The truth will set you free! It is important to acknowledge that you are angry. Using denial to hide your anger is a temporary fix, not a long-term solution. The myths people learn about anger (nice people don't get angry) causes them to ignore their feelings that, like flashing red lights, warn them of impending danger. Unacknowledged anger will cause you physical, psychological, and spiritual problems that can be long lasting. People with depression and substance abuse problems often carry their unacknowledged anger like a torch they refuse to relinquish.

Unacknowledged anger takes on its own life. It becomes a separate parasitic entity that can suck the life out of you. God revealed to me that if you take each letter in the word *A.N.G.E.R*, and separate it, you will find that anger is like an:

*A*nchor that keeps you bound to pain and suffering and does not allow you to love freely

*N*egating God's help to free you from the chains of loneliness and pain, and becomes a

*G*od in your life, taking control over you and the

*E*nergy needed for more positive endeavors, preventing a

*R*eunification of your spirit with God's

What does the acronym *A.N.G.E.R* mean to you? _____

_____

_____

What would happen if you were to acknowledge that you are angry? _____

_____

_____

You deny your anger because _____

_____

_____

Confess your anger:

Acknowledging your faults opens the door to change, confessing them leads to the inner court of change.

— Nola Veazie

Confession is good for the soul! The bible tells us to confess our trespasses and pray for one another so we don't fall into temptation. Angry people tend to deny that they are angry, as if it is not written all over their faces. You don't have to go up on your rooftop and shout, "I'm an angry person." However, telling God that you are angry gives Him permission to bring freedom to your soul. It is a humbling experience when you confess your weaknesses to another person or even to God. Telling someone else that there is a flaw in you can produce anxiety, but can also bring you freedom.

The great leaders in the bible weren't great because they were without sin; they were great because they confessed their sin. David, a man after God's heart, committed adultery; Moses, who led God's people out of captivity, was a murderer; Paul, who was a self-proclaimed prisoner in chains for the gospel, persecuted God's people; Peter, a great disciple of Jesus, denied knowing Him. Each and every one of these great men exhibited shortcomings, some worse than others. However, their moment of freedom and greatness came when they humbled themselves and confessed their sin.

Do you find yourself harboring un-confessed anger that threatens to destroy your relationship with others and with God? If so, take this opportunity to say the following prayer:

Dear Lord, your word says that it is the little foxes (things in life) that spoil the vine (our connection to you); I pray that you shine your light through me and uncover any anger that may have taken up residence there. I confess feeling: _____ towards: _____ forgive me. I pray that you will touch _____ heart so he/she will also forgive me. I will not bring my sacrifice before you unless I first forgive my brother/sister.

My personal prayer: _____

_____
_____
_____
_____
_____
_____
_____
_____
_____
_____
_____
_____
_____
_____
_____
_____
_____
_____
_____
_____
_____
_____
_____
_____
_____
_____
_____
_____
_____
_____
_____
_____
_____
_____
_____
_____
_____

Trust God for the ability to regulate your anger:

Asking an angry person to trust is like asking a doughnut lover to give up Krispy Kreams. Trust eludes a number of people due to hurts and misunderstandings they've encountered earlier in life. The build up of your anger creates a wall between you and others, sometimes even blocking God's love. The wall of anger you create greatly diminishes your capacity to open up and receive healing.

Understand, anger ultimately only hurts you. Why build something that will eventually tear you down? The bible asks us to *trust in the Lord with all our heart and not to lean on our understanding of things.* When you are hurt, it is hard to see things clearly, causing you to skew reality. Your anger tells you that others are bad or have bad intentions; it also causes a mental fog that cast a shadow of negativity on life. The last time you were angry, can you recall thinking good thoughts towards the other person? Can you recall thinking good things about yourself?

As I stated earlier, anger cast a shadow of darkness over situations in life and makes them seem insurmountable. The bible says that *God is the lamp that enlightens your darkness* (2 Sam 22:29). When your anger comes down like a dark veil that makes your path obscure, remember that the word of God is a lamp to your feet and a light to your path. His word will guide you out of the darkness of unregulated anger, but you must trust Him to do it.

Perhaps you have suffered from some form of abuse perpetrated by someone you should have been able to trust, leaving you angry and unable to trust God. Take this opportunity to meditate on the scriptures that tell you that *God is not a man that He should lie; and that He loves you with an everlasting love.*

My ability to trust has been shaken by: _____

_____

_____

_____

_____

Uproot the bitterness

Blessed are the peacemakers, for they shall be called sons of God.

_Matthew 5:9

Jesus often spoke in parables and compared his Kingdom to a field sown with good seeds, but the enemy came in when no one was watching and sowed tares among the wheat. Anger is like tares that grow and eventually overrun the seeds of love and trust planted in your heart. The bible says that at the harvest, the farmer gathered the tares and burned them. Likewise, you can gather every angry thought that consumes you and symbolically burn them.

Allowing the roots of bitterness to grow in your heart will kill your ability to love. As a part-time gardener, I've allowed one or two weeds to grow in the garden. I was busy and did not think they would become a huge problem. I must say that it did not take long before the weeds took over. I felt overwhelmed and did not have the energy to invest in getting rid of them, to the detriment of my garden. Before you know it, little seeds of anger can grow and become big roots of bitterness, embedded in your heart. Trying to separate the good roots from the bad ones can be an insurmountable task. Don't wait until the garden of your heart is overrun by bitterness; give God permission to uproot them so that the good seed will grow freely.

How do you uproot bitterness? Experience has taught me that it is easier to uproot weeds when the ground is moist. Trying to dig up weeds from hard, dry ground is almost impossible. I've tried! Likewise, when your heart is hard and dry from life's drought, digging up bitterness becomes challenging. Has your heart become hard and dry like the ground in the desert? Don't despair. The bible says in Ezekiel that God will give you a new heart and put a new spirit in you. He will take the heart of stone out of your flesh and replace it with a heart of flesh.

Your new supple heart will make it easy to uproot any bitterness and allow God's love to penetrate. In order to receive this heart transplant, you must pray.

Pray

Pray without ceasing (1 Thessalonians 5:17). Prayer is more than communication with God; it keeps you connected to the source of nutrition and help, the vine! How many times have you heard the phrase, "prayer changes things"? People say it in such a casual way; they minimize its true power and reduce it to a cliché! Prayer does change things. It changes your situation, your behavior, and it even changes the way you think.

How can prayer regulate your anger? I mentioned earlier in this chapter that your anger can potentially become a god that ultimately takes control over your life. Prayer puts your anger in perspective and reminds you that God is all-powerful, not your anger. Prayer calms your anxieties and gives you the *peace of God, which baffles your understanding* (Phil 4:6-7).

Anger covers emotions that would otherwise make you feel vulnerable. When you communicate with God through prayer, you grant Him access to those emotions and give Him permission to heal them. Uncovering hurt and disappointments gives you the opportunity to openly deal with them, minimizing their power and your need to protect them with anger.

Prayer also gives you the opportunity to speak things out loud and challenge irrational thinking. You may say that you don't pray audibly. Even when you pray in your mind, you can hear yourself and sometimes you are able to ascertain if the thoughts that reinforce your anger are irrational.

How do you pray? Jesus left an example in the book of Matthew that not only teaches you to pray, but puts the reason for prayer in perspective. Prayer acknowledges God's supremacy; it is the vehicle used to establish a connection to God; prayer is a request for His will in your life; it allows forgiveness to flow from God, through you, to others; prayer reminds you that it is God who keeps you from falling into temptation. The most important aspect of the role of prayer in regulating your anger is asking God for the strength to forgive.

Meditate on the model prayer found in Matthew 6.

Our Father in heaven: God wants a personal relationship with you; the same desired relationship parents long to have with their children.

Hallowed be your name: His name must be elevated above all other names.

Your kingdom come: Ask for God's order in heaven to be accomplished on earth.

Your will be done: God's desire for your life should prevail over your desires.

On earth as it is in heaven: What goes on in heaven should be duplicated on earth.

Give us this day our daily bread: God supplies your daily spiritual, physical, and emotional needs.

And forgive us our debts: The trespasses and angry feelings that indebt you to others.

As we forgive our debtors: You must forgive those who hurt you.

And do not lead us into temptation: God will not lead you into slippery places.

But deliver us from the evil one: God will save you from the grip of the enemy (even from your anger).

For Yours is the kingdom and the power and the glory forever and ever: The word of God says that the kingdom is in us and among us; it is not just food or drink, but every good thing we desire. God has the power to do all things always, amen.

My prayer today is _____

Chapter 5

THE CLOUD OF WITNESSES

The bible refers to biblical role models as a great cloud of witnesses. These are ordinary people whose lives were highlighted because they overcame adversity and their faith grew stronger, people who learned a great lesson because of conquering anger and resentment. They gained victory over their emotions, taking back the lives they loss for a period of time. These witnesses are regular people like you who maintained confidence in God's ability to help them overcome trials and tribulations. The book of Hebrews points out that these individuals serve as a great cloud of witnesses (role models) for our learning. Their stories serve as examples for subsequent generations that would endure and overcome sin, "let us lay aside every weight and sin which so easily traps us."

There are many people whose life experiences serve as models from which we gain strength to deal with unspeakable situations that result from anger. These are everyday people living normal lives who, like you, allowed anger to take control. Their stories may not be broadcast on television or even talked about; nevertheless, it impacted their lives and the lives of people close to them. These are the people who allowed their anger to rule for a period of time, but through God's grace and mercy learned to regulate it, thereby changing the course of their lives. They chose to be thermostats instead of thermometers (See Chapter 3).

Out of the cloud appears a ray of sunlight, the story of two individuals whose experience with anger serves as a witness for all of us. Their stories speak to the goodness and mercy of God and remind us that He has placed in us the ability to deal with life's problems without allowing anger to reign. His holy spirit guides us and intercedes on our behalf, keeping us from falling into temptation, instead making a way of escape. God's spirit prompts us to ask for wisdom, self-control, temperance, and above all, the principle thing, Love!

Each remarkable story in this book is spoken from the person's own descent into darkness and later their ascent to victory over unregulated anger. The names have been changed, but the situations are real, the agony is real, and so is their triumph. Maybe you can identify with each person's story, or there is a little bit of each person in you; I pray that you realize that God's power is sufficient for you; in your weakness He is strong.

Nadia's Song

"The eye-catching array of spring blooms announced the beginning of a beautiful day in May 1980. Each note sung by the birds came together in a harmonious display of musical colors. If you closed your eyes you could almost see the hues across the European sky. Spain was particularly sunny that day, with a slight crisp chill in the air that crystallized the musical notes sung by the birds and the colors from the flower garden. Looking back, it was as if the chill captured the colors and sounds, like the matting that frames a painting. I would summarize the beauty of that day as the kind you desire to capture in your mind, like a picture you pass on from generation to generation."

"Instinctively, I noticed the mood of the day changing! As in the calm before the storm, I felt serene but then the build-up of tension came down like a shadow over me. The calm I experienced was similar to the calm in the eye of a hurricane; but when it passed, the disturbing force of my anger gave way to disaster. I suddenly realized that I held a four-inch blade in my hand that pierced the soft colors of that day and replaced them with the deep red color of blood. In one fail swoop, anger turned my song into a sad story. No longer were the birds singing or the rays from the sun shinning and drizzling gold tones on the flowers and fairy dust on people passing by."

"One thoughtless move with the four inch blade of a knife turned the light of my day into the blackest night! Who turned out the light? The question appeared in my mind like a ghost that was lurking, waiting to materialize one day. My anger jumped out of the shadows and took center stage without an invitation. This is my story, one shared by many others who allowed anger to reign for a moment. The word of God says that weeping may endure for a night, but joy comes in the morning. Some mornings it seems like the reverse is true, that weeping endures a lifetime, along with the darkness of the night."

"My story does not begin with this awful event, it starts with my pain. What can I say about myself? I was married at a young age and entertained all the same fantasies most young married women do. I wanted two children, a loving and successful husband, and a career. I never gave much thought about any particular vocation, I just wanted to be successful at whatever I did. My life was similar to any other young working mom, juggling the responsibilities of work, motherhood and being a wife. I was different than other wives and mothers in one way, I carried a tomb full of the dead bones of repressed anger and pain."

"My anger lay dormant for many years, peaking to the surface once in a while when someone or something provoked it, like bait coaxing it out of the dark waters. Repressed anger, hmmm, sounds like some rare disorder found in a psychology book, but it is not. Repressed anger, I found out, is simply anger that is locked in the closet of your mind, not easily accessible, or so I thought. Something that is hidden for so long seems strange when it appears. Anger was no stranger to me, yet, that day, I hardly recognized it. I remember the pain tumbling out of my heart, wrapped in this familiar stranger called anger."

"Before that faithful day, my lifelong goal was to succeed in the workplace. I could hardly identify the energy that seemingly fueled my drive, but it kept me striving so I did not rock the boat. The same energy also kept me from reaching deeper depths of intimacy in my relationship. It energized me just enough to maintain the status quo, but not enough to want to go to that place of oneness in my relationship. I never questioned my inability to go to that place, but I knew that something had to give. I never thought that that something would be me. Reaching the breaking point exposed the intensity of my anger; it also brought to the surface the amount of pain I concealed."

"You know things were good for awhile, I can't pinpoint the moment they changed. Now that I think about it, I do know when things changed! The situation seemed different when the thought came to my mind that I was a throw away child. What do I mean by a throw away child? The vulnerable child in all of us, left unattended or pushed to the side by the people who professes to love them. In my case, it is the child who is left by her Father. You would think that all these years later, I would not long for my dad, but all children long for their father."

"Somehow it feels like this story has nothing to do with my husband! I think it has more to do with the hole left by my dad; at times my pain seems very confusing, I don't always recognize it's source. The lack of intimacy and trust in my marriage revealed my longing for a relationship with my father. This void led to the emotional breakup that preceded the physical breakup of the relationship; I realized that the pain came from one source—abandonment from both my father and my husband."

"My husband John began to drift away from me and move towards drugs and other women. His emotional exodus soon turned into a physical one, leaving me feeling abandoned and helpless. The more I think about it, the more he reminds me of my father, but that is another story. I remember clearly the first time I saw him with that other woman. She represented something more in my mind than another woman; I just did not know it at the time. I don't know if anyone else can relate to the feelings she represented in my mind, a void left by my father, abandonment! I guess I will refer to her as Abandonment."

"I felt the sadness come over me like a mist, making it difficult to see with clarity. Looking back I can see why my thoughts were so jumbled! My husband John and Abandonment, his new mistress, began to consume my every thought. I often found myself thinking: What are they doing? Where is he? What is her hold on him? The question I should have asked was the following: What is her hold on me? I did not realize she kept a strong grip on one side while anger (my partner) held on tight on the other side. The force of the two pulling me in opposite directions, at times, almost tore me apart." "What drives a person to this point?"

"Sadly, I finally succumbed to the force exerted by abandonment and anger. For a long time all I remembered, was holding the knife in my hand while my husband was bleeding to death. I've since regained more memories of that faithful day. John was getting ready to go out to meet his mistress. I tried to stop John. I begged him not to leave me. His vacant look reinforced the thought in my head that I was a throw away child, one who is easily discarded. Suddenly, my partner (anger) spoke up and said, take control, don't let his mistress (abandonment) win this battle, and I snapped. That sunny spring day turned into a chilling and bloody afternoon, one I will never forget as long as I live."

"God's grace is sufficient! John, lived to tell the authorities what really happened; my intentions were not to kill him, I wanted to stop him from going to his mistress. The pain of losing him, at the time, was reminiscent of the pain of not having my father. John told me that he remembered me grabbing the knife from the counter (I was in a daze, having an out-of-body experience). He said that I was screaming and crying and waving the knife as he tried to stop me; unfortunately, during the struggle for the knife it penetrated his neck. The knife reached within half of one inch of his jugular, but did not puncture it nor caused permanent damage. I allowed my feelings of abandonment to fuel my anger and dictate my behavior; the power I gave to my anger almost took a life."

"Anger can take us to a place we would rather not go. It turned me into a person I did not recognize or want to be; I've since learned to manage my anger, in fact, I've learned to manage my thoughts. **I'm no longer controlled by anger nor abandonment; neither am I controlled by relationships with those who do not want a relationship with me."**

"The word of God says that He will restore the years the locust has eaten; in this case the locust was my anger. God's faithfulness filtered through the anger and allowed a ray of light to reach those dark and broken places in my heart. I finally realized that I had the power of forgiveness. I had the power to regulate the heat of anger and release myself from the ties of abandonment. God's mercy and grace did not allow John to die nor did it allow me to spend the rest of my life in jail. Instead, God taught me to accept His forgiveness and give it to others."

Points for discussion

Nadia's anger was secondary to the feelings of abandonment she experienced growing up without a father. The same feelings resurfaced during her relationship with her husband.

1. What other underlying (primary) feelings did you see after reading the story?
2. What led Nadia to stab her husband?
3. At what point in the story did Nadia become a thermostat?
4. Can you identify the process of change in her life?
5. How does this story relate to your situation?

Victoria's Secret: The Bed of Venom

The word venom conjures many images, all related to poison and death. Victoria's story is one that could have ended in spiritual death, but as the word of God professes, the end of a thing is better than the beginning. Victoria likened this chapter of her life to a journey into a bed of venom, a pit full of destructive snakes waiting to inject her with their paralyzing and deadly substance. "I was injected, with the type of venom that is far more insidious than the venom of a snake; one that slowly infects every fiber of your being until it takes full control of all that is good and pure in you, the venom of anger!"

"I became cognizant of my inner struggle, when I first realized that my fairytale marriage never existed. The marriage that was supposed to be a fantasy was instead a nightmare. My husband was addicted to many things, but I was not one of them. We started our married life with a lie, one that became the theme throughout our marriage; when you have told a lie, you continue telling it because you lose track of the truth."

"I've heard that there is no wrath like the one of a woman scorned. I guess it is true! The anger I felt when I found out about my husband's lies made me want to hurt him. The problem with anger is that you sometimes turn it inside and hurt yourself; my anger was like a fire I kept near me, I could not avoid being burn. I often said mean and hurtful things to him, sometimes the verbal attacks escalated into physical struggles, trying to get him to wake up and change. Instead, I became depressed and unable to function."

"I needed to find a way to cope with my pain, and denial became the comfort I needed; it was not long however, before I replaced denial with anger, my new friend. At my lowest level, anger moved up in rank until it replaced God in my life. My prayer life began to suffer, but there were people around who could pray for me. I was filled with shame and guilt because of the intensity of my anger, and inability to overcome my problems. My feelings of anger towards my husband consumed every thought and soon permeated every fiber of my being. Who is this person in the mirror? I hardly recognized myself anymore. It was as if this feeling that took over me changed the way I looked."

"I remember the callousness that covered and numbed my feelings towards my husband. It was as if my soul was hardened and covered the goodness in me, but it did not stop me from trying to love others. The venom of anger injected in me caused me much pain. The only way I found relief was to inflict that pain on my husband. It is interesting, the rejection I felt was similar to what I experienced in grade school. The other kids made fun of my strong European accent, my appearance, and my style. All the feelings from years past rushed back and I suddenly felt like a yo-yo on a string, spinning out of control only to be re-wrapped in anger."

"The details of my husband's misgivings are not important; the way I allowed my anger to control me is. As I said earlier in my story, my lowest point was allowing anger to become a God in my life. I lost perspective; I forgot that others in my life depended on me; I did not remember the people who loved me and were praying for me; I could not help myself or anyone else. Sadly, I lost temporary contact with my creator!"

"Anger consumed me in such a way, I could not think of anyone else. I forgot that other people had problems; I also forgot that I was part of the World. I created my own World, full of pain and hopelessness. I became so depressed I could not get out of bed; I no longer had the energy to carry on. The emotional toll was devastating for me and those who watched me sink into despair."

"Have you ever loved someone with eyes wide open? Anger either keeps you from loving or it closes your eyes to the truth, the truth about yourself. Coming face to face with the pain of rejection was not easy, but even harder is facing the angry person I became. The reflection I saw in the mirror was that of a person who no longer acknowledge the good in someone else, a person who sees only the bad things about others and criticizes them. I constantly criticized my husband, hoping it would motivate him to change. Of course criticism and anger does not motivate anyone to change, it only made me more angry."

"The shame I felt caused my the reflection in the mirror became my wakeup call. It allowed me to see that I gave my anger permission to steal the most precious thing in my life, my relationship with God. I find it ironic that the more time I invested in trying to change my husband, the less time I spent with God."

"The dawning of a new day is here! I've escaped the bed of venom and chosen to take the seat of forgiveness. I've since forgiven my husband and released him from the chains I placed around his neck with my anger. My completion is not in him, but it is in God, the author and finisher of my faith. I learned that I was fearfully and wonderfully made and that God's thoughts were on me before my beginning. It is a great revelation to know that I have a comforter who gives me a sense of security when I'm afraid, who loves me when I'm unlovable, who reflects the true me when I'm blinded by my anger."

Points for discussion

Victoria, like many others internalized her anger and it manifested in the form of depression. A lack of appropriate coping skills can lead to avoidance of feelings; seek help from a professional if you find yourself experiencing the following symptoms: Insomnia or too much sleep, decreased appetite, low energy, lack of interest in friends or activities you previously enjoyed, thoughts of death or suicide.

1. What fueled Victoria's anger?
2. Would you consider her a thermostat or thermometer?
3. Can you identify with her story?
4. What would you do differently?
5. What would you do the same?

Do you find yourself in any of the stories on the previous page? If you do you are not alone. A number of people allow anger to take them to places they wish they could forget. The dark places of regret, unforgiveness, defeat, helplessness, and hopelessness, but you do not have to stay in those places because God gives you power to regulate your anger.

On a scale from 1 to 10 where is your anger? It may range from a score of 1 (irritability) to a 10 (rage), changing in intensity according to the way you feel or think about the situation. Complete the daily journal on the following page by first circling the intensity of your anger and filling in the blank lines with the situation, your belief about the situation or person, if you acted like a thermostat or thermometer, and finally emotional, physical, or spiritual consequences.

Monday
Intensity 1 2 3 4 5 6 7 8 9 10
Situation _____

_____

_____

My thoughts _____

_____

_____

Did I act like a thermostat or a thermometer? _____

_____

_____

Consequence _____

_____

_____

My prayer _____

_____

_____

Verse to remember: *You will keep him in perfect peace, whose mind is stayed on you* (Isa 26:3).

Tuesday
Intensity 1 2 3 4 5 6 7 8 9 10
Situation————————————————————————————

—————————————————————————————————————
—————————————————————————————————————

My thoughts ——————————————————————————

—————————————————————————————————————

Did I act like a thermostat or a thermometer? —————

—————————————————————————————————————

Consequence——————————————————————————

—————————————————————————————————————

My prayer ————————————————————————————

—————————————————————————————————————

Verse to remember: *Let all bitterness, wrath, anger, clamor and evil speaking be put away from you, with all malice* (Eph 4:31).

Wednesday
Intensity 1 2 3 4 5 6 7 8 9 10
Situation _____

_____

_____

My thoughts _____

_____

_____

Did I act like a thermostat or a thermometer? _____

_____

_____

Consequence _____

_____

_____

My prayer _____

_____

_____

Verse to remember: *Be angry and do not sin, do not let the sun go down on your wrath* (Eph 4:26).

Thursday
Intensity 1 2 3 4 5 6 7 8 9 10
Situation_____

_____
_____

My thoughts _____

_____
_____

Did I act like a thermostat or a thermometer? _____

_____
_____

Consequence_____

_____
_____

My prayer_____

_____
_____

Verse to remember: *Hatred stirs up strife, but love covers all sins* (Prov 10:12).

Friday

Intensity 1 2 3 4 5 6 7 8 9 10

Situation _____

_____

_____

My thoughts _____

_____

_____

Did I act like a thermostat or a thermometer? _____

_____

_____

Consequence _____

_____

_____

My prayer _____

_____

_____

Verse to remember: *Your word is a lamp to my feet and a light to my path* (Psa 119:105).

Saturday
Intensity 1 2 3 4 5 6 7 8 9 10
Situation_____

_____

_____

My thoughts _____

_____

_____

Did I act like a thermostat or a thermometer? _____

_____

_____

Consequence_____

_____

_____

My prayer _____

_____

_____

Verse to remember: *For God has not given us a spirit of fear, but of power and of love and of a sound mind* (2 Tim 1:7).

Sunday
Intensity 1 2 3 4 5 6 7 8 9 10
Situation _____
_____
_____

My thoughts _____
_____
_____

Did I act like a thermostat or a thermometer? _____
_____
_____

Consequence _____._____
_____
_____

My prayer _____
_____
_____

Verse to remember: *Avoid foolish and ignorant arguments, knowing that they generate strife* (2 Tim 2:23).

Chapter 6

THE MEDITATIONS OF YOUR HEART

I t is impossible to sustain two opposing feelings; you cannot be happy and sad or angry and glad at the same time, at least not for a long period of time. Even if you are talented enough to summon both feelings, dedicating mental energy to both is emotionally difficult; the feeling that is strongest will prevail-the one you dedicate the most mental energy to!

The word of God tells you to meditate on things that are inspirational; that nurtures your spirit and brings prosperity to your soul; in other words, dedicate your mental energy to thoughts that are emotionally healthy. An example of this is found in the book of Philippians 4:8, "finally brethren, whatever things are true, whatever things are noble, whatever things are just, whatever things are pure, whatever things are lovely, whatever things are of good report, if there is any virtue and if there is anything praiseworthy-meditate on these things."

The above verse is part of a letter sent by Paul to the Philippians exhorting them to imitate his behavior, by nourishing their thoughts with meditations that are uplifting. Paul's writings underline his understanding of the connection between his thinking and his mood and consequently his behavior; he shared these teachings in the book of Philippians, underscoring the need to keep his thoughts on godly things in order to gain the peace of God.

Paul often found himself in situations that seemed hopeless and beyond his ability to cope; the scripture makes mention of his suffering referring to it as a thorn in his flesh; in spite of his afflictions, Paul was able to meditate on God's grace and the word of God that kept him from falling into despair. Feeding your mind with negative thoughts such as: "I should be over this by now"; "I can't trust anyone", "God does not hear me", "God does not love me", "I'm too bad to be loved", only reinforces a sense of hopelessness and helplessness and increases negative feelings.

In chapter three I stated that your thinking (the meditations of your heart) influences and drives your behavior (as a man thinks of himself so is he; or, that is what he becomes). I illustrated how your belief or way of thinking, not events in your life, is ultimately responsible for your anger and the way you respond to others.

Let's use Jim's interaction (from chapter 3) with the teller at his bank to illustrate the above statement. This time I will change his "stinking thinking" by incorporating the word of God.

Activating event: Teller closed the window as Jim approached her.

Belief system: "I know all things work together for the good of those who are called according to the purpose of God." "Standing in line a little longer until another teller opens the window, gives me an opportunity to meditate on God's word." "It also gives me an opportunity to get rid of my anxiety by taking a deep breath to relax."

Consequence: Jim is more relaxed and able to have positive interactions with those around him, including the next teller.

The result of Jim's interaction with the teller was more positive and led to a better outcome. The difference in outcome was directly linked to Jim's positive appraisal of the situation, and the choice he made to meditate on God's word instead of ruminating about his negative feelings. Jim was also able to challenge his irrational thinking that previously caused him to conclude that the teller was out to get him. Now that you are aware of how your negative thinking influences your mood and ultimately your behavior, how do you change it? The word change may set off alarm bells in your mind that sends you running for cover; you may ask yourself, how do I purge my mind from negative thinking? Can I erase the old tapes that have played in my mind over and over for many years? These questions are not easily answered; you must first recognize that your negative thinking is a result of a lifetime of recorded tapes.

I liken the recording of thought processes to the recording of lyrics on an old tape player (those of you born in the CD and DVD era won't know what I'm talking about). The ideas and teachings you hear and learn from your family, books, television, friends, including environmental influences, are recorded in your mind and are played back in response to a given situation; these recorded tapes are played over and over, in similar situations, until they become an automatic part of your response, and later your belief system. Once embedded, this new belief system is difficult to erase; the only way to remove it is to tape over it!

Erasing negative or irrational thinking is a two-fold process: 1. Challenge the irrational thought, which promotes negative feelings 2. Meditate on information that sustains healthy thinking, such as the word of God and positive affirmations. Challenging irrational thinking can be difficult if you do not recognize the thought as irrational; for example, thinking that a situation will never change is irrational. Why is it irrational? Change is inevitable; season's change, people change (slowly), and situations change. On the other hand, meditating on information that sustains healthy thinking seems easier; after all, we are part of the communication super highway; information travels at the speed of light across the Internet and the media. Unfortunately, this information is not always uplifting and can be counterproductive. Finding information that is uplifting can prove to be a challenge.

Where do you find information that will inspire you? How does it become a part of your thinking? The word of God is a source of inspiration that gives you access to life changing information; when you read and meditate on the word of God, you will find comfort (Psalms and Proverbs), motivation (Ephesians and Philippians), it builds your self-esteem (Psalms), answers questions about life (Genesis and Revelation), and most importantly it contains the thoughts of your Creator towards you; an example of this is found in Jeremiah 29:11 ("For I know the thoughts that I think toward you, says the Lord, thoughts of peace and not of evil, to give you a future and a hope").

Incorporating or establishing a new belief system requires practice. Your current belief system did not happen overnight; I've heard people say that if you hear something more than once, you believe it to be true. Unfortunately, this is not far from the truth; if you tell yourself over and over that your angry disposition protects you from others, you will eventually believe it. In like manner, if you tell yourself that God is your present help in times of need, you will also believe that God truly will be there in your time of need.

Acquiring and using more positive thinking is a choice; the difference between people who act like a thermostat versus those who act like thermometers is the former recognizes he/she has the power of choice and opts to use that power. For example, the thermostat chooses to carry and use the shield of faith to protect him/her from the fiery darts of the enemy; he/she dons the helmet of salvation as a safeguard against negative thinking that incite anger. On the other hand, the thermometer becomes a victim of his/her thinking; this person fails to see the choices available to him/her.

What is the shield of faith? The bible defines faith in the book of Hebrews as the substance of things that we hope for, the evidence of things we are not yet able to see. When you board a plane you hope to get to your destination, but are unable to see signs or markers from 35,000 feet up in the air; nevertheless, you hope that the pilot knows how to get you there and believe that he will. Likewise the person who thinks like a thermostat knows that Jesus is the pilot in charge of his situation and is able to get him the desired result—even when you cannot see the outcome in advance! The shield of faith is the knowledge that Jesus will intercede on your behalf, if you ask him; it protects you from the type of thinking that sustains bitterness.

The helmet of salvation is a reminder of the great price Jesus paid to save you. A thermostat uses his helmet of salvation to guard against negative thinking that suggests he/she is worthless or stupid. These cognitive appraisals about self and others create a mental picture that sustains angry feelings. On the other hand, when you think about yourself as heir to the kingdom through salvation you see yourself in a position of power, reigning over anger.

You must practice this line of thinking in order that it become a part of your belief system; reading about faith or the helmet of salvation will not help you if you do not repeat it until you believe it. When faced with a troublesome situation, you will need these tools at your immediate disposal.

How do you know when your thinking has changed to that of a thermostat? Change can be a slow process; nevertheless, there are a few subtle clues that tell you that you are transitioning from thermometer to thermostat thinking. You begin to recognize that your thinking causes you to react like a thermometer (reacting to your emotions and the behavior of others); you consciously decide to be a thermostat, and thus regulate your anger/emotions; you choose to (ACT-UP) Acknowledge that you are angry, Confess your anger, Trust God to help you with your anger, Uproot bitterness from your heart, and Pray not to use your anger as a shield. What is the next step? The next step is simple! Make the choice to use God's word as the source of your meditations; this enables you to tape over the thinking that previously sustained your anger.

The following is a test of your new thermostat thinking.

Record a situation in which you reacted like a thermometer:

Using the ACT-UP model record the following information:

I **Acknowledged** my anger by:

I **Confessed** that I was angry to:

I showed **Trust** in God by:

I know that I **Uprooted** the bitterness in my heart because:

My **Prayer** is the following:

How would you handle the situation differently? In other words, more like a thermostat!

Meditating on things that are good and wholesome inspires positive thinking; it also mitigates angry feelings and puts you in a better mood. The following pages are filled with words of inspiration and poems for your meditation pleasure.

THINK ON THESE THINGS

- Things That Are Pure

- Things That Are Noble

- Things That Are Just

- Things That Are Lovely

- Things That Are Of Good Report

Following each meditation you will find a blank page to journal your thoughts. Meditating on things that are uplifting is not always easy; you are often bombarded with negative news and the negative thinking of angry people. Changing your thinking takes practice, doing the journals gives you the opportunity to practice.

Things That Are Pure

Peace

Grace

God's Agape love

Fresh mountain air

The first rain of spring

The scent of a newborn baby

Love without pretense or conditions

It is often difficult to think about the beauty of God's creation when you are overwhelmed by the demands of daily living; you may rush from point A to point B, seldom recognizing the need to stop and take a breath. When was the last time you meditated on something that is pure? Perhaps you live in the city and don't have the benefit of breathing fresh mountain air, or experiencing the first rain of spring. Can you enjoy God's agape love where you are?

God's Agape Love
"For God so loved the world that He gave His only begotten Son, that whoever believes in Him should not perish but have everlasting life." __John 3:16

Agape love is the kind of love that gives, it asks nothing in return; a love that believes in you and your worth to the point of giving itself. When was the last time someone died so that you can live?

"Hatred stirs up strife, but love covers all sins."__ Proverbs 10:12

Love frees you from the chains of anger and bitterness; it is the key to liberty. Hatred chains you to the person it is directed towards. Are you willing to be bound to someone for life, when the bond that ties you comes from hatred?

"And now abide faith, hope, love, these three; but the greatest of these is love." __I Corinthians 13:13

In life we must have hope for the future and faith in God, but it is love that sustains the first two.

"Now the purpose of the commandment is love from a pure heart, from a good conscience, and from sincere faith." __I Timothy 1:5

Love from a pure heart requires making yourself vulnerable to others; few people achieve this level of love because few people are willing to risk it.

Peace
"Blessed are the peacemakers, for they shall be called sons of God." __Matthew 5:9

Peace is such a pure thing that God gave the privilege of becoming sons and daughters to those who seek it.

"Depart from evil and do good; seek peace, and pursue It." __Psalm 34:14

To pursue peace means to follow it in order to overtake and capture it!

"And let the peace of God rule in your hearts, to which also you were called in one body." __Colossians 3:15

Open up your heart so that the peace of God may capture it.

"Peace be within your walls, prosperity within your palaces." __Psalm 122:7

Does peace dwell within the walls of your mind?

"These things I have spoken unto you that in me you might have peace." __John 16:33

The word of God is spoken into your heart that you might have peace in your mind.

**"You will keep him in perfect peace, whose mind is stayed
on you; because he trust in you." __Isaiah 26:3**

Keeping your mind on Christ, keeps peace in it!

**"Great peace have those who love your law, and nothing
causes them to stumble." __Psalm 119:165**

Peace is like the light bulb that comes on in your mind as a
result of obedience to God's law.

My Journal Of Things That Are Pure

Things That Are Just

God's statutes

God's word

Mercy

Freedom

Helping someone

Showing mercy

It is tempting to say that nothing in life is just or fair; maybe your life experiences have left you bitter and resentful or sad and not being able to trust. People and situations, at times, may let you down; the word of God tells us that he is the same yesterday, today and tomorrow. It also tells us that God is not a man that he should tell a lie; if the word of God said He is just, it is true. God is just!

God's Word

**"Your word is a lamp to my fee and a light to my path"
__Psalm 119:105**

Anger often comes down like a dark veil covering and obscuring the path you should take; meditating on God's word enlightens your path and gives clarity to the situation.

**"Your word I have hidden in my heart, that I might not sin against you."
__Psalm 119:11**

Record the word of God in your heart that you may have a tool to counter the enemy of your mind.

**"The grass withers, the flower fades, but the word of our God stands forever."
__Isaiah 40:8**

Earthly things, including fads, disappear with time; the word of God is a mainstay that never fades or goes out of style.

"But whoever keeps His word, truly the love of God is perfected in him. By this we know that we are in Him." — I John 2:5

Justice is found in the word of God, whoever keeps God's statutes will find it.

Freedom

"Therefore if the son makes you free, you shall be free indeed." __John 8:36

If Jesus sets you free, why bind yourself with unforgiveness and hatred?

"Stand fast therefore in the liberty by which Christ has made us free, and do not be entangled again with a yoke of bondage." __Galatians 5:1

Why go back and rehash old arguments that rekindle anger?

"For the law of the spirit of life in Christ Jesus has made me free from the law of sin and death." __Romans 8:2

The price paid for your freedom was great; enjoy it!

Mercy

"Oh give thanks to the Lord, for he is good! For his mercy endures forever."
__I Chronicles 16:34

Be thankful for God's unmerited favor towards you.

"I trust in the mercy of God forever and ever." Psalm 52:8
"But God, who is rich in mercy, because of his great love with which he loved us, even when we were dead in trespasses, made us alive together with Christ." __
Ephesians 2:4

God's mercy saved you from sure death.

"Let us therefore come boldly to the throne of grace, that we may obtain mercy and find grace to help in time of need." __Hebrews 4:16

Thank God that there is a place where you can go to obtain mercy

My Journal Of
Things That Are Just

Things That Are True

Salvation is free

You will not always be sad

God's safety and provision

You are created in God's image

There is a time under the sun for everything

God's thoughts are of peace and hope towards you

You've probably heard the saying—nothing in life is free! You may believe that you don't get something for nothing; when someone does something for you, they are expecting something in return. There is one gift that comes without any strings attached—God's Salvation!

There Is A Time Under The Sun For Everything
__Ecclesiastes 3:1-8

To everything there is a season,
A time for every purpose
Under heaven:
A time to be born,
And a time to die;
A time to plant,
And a time to pluck what is planted:
A time to kill,
And a time to heal;
A time to break down,
And a time to build up;
A time to weep,
And a time to laugh;
A time to mourn,
And a time to dance;
A time to cast away stones,
And a time to gather stones;
A time to embrace,
And a time to refrain from embracing;
A time to gain,
And a time to lose;
A time to keep,
And a time to throw away;
A time to tear,
And a time to sew;
A time to keep silence,
And a time to speak;

**A time to love,
And a time to hate;
A time of war,
And a time of peace.**

Salvation Is Free

But we are bound to give thanks to God always for you, brethren beloved by the Lord, because God from the beginning chose you for salvation through sanctification by the spirit and belief in the truth." __II Thessalonians 2:13

God chose you for salvation without any prerequisite.

"The Lord is my light and my salvation; whom shall I fear?

God is your salvation!

"Salvation belongs to the Lord. Your blessing is upon your people."

It is not by your own doing that you are saved, but by the mercy of God.

"And Moses said to the people, do not be afraid; stand still, and see the salvation of the Lord..." __Exodus14:13

If you do not stand still, it is difficult to focus on the beauty of God's salvation.

God's Safety And Provision

"The Lord is my shepherd; I shall not want. He makes me to lie down in green pastures; He leads me beside the still waters. He restores my soul; He leads me in the paths of righteousness for His name's sake. Yea, though I walk through the valley of the shadow of death, I will fear no evil; for you are with me; your rod and your staff, they comfort me. You prepare a table before me in the presence of my enemies; you anoint my head with oil; my cup runs over. Surely goodness and mercy shall follow me all the days of my life; and I will dwell in the house of the Lord forever." __Psalm 23

Anger and other negative emotions often spring from fear, worry, and doubt. Losing your income can cause you to doubt God's ability to provide safety and security for your family, but it does not change His position as Lord.

"The Lord is my shepherd, I shall not want."

John 10:11 tell us that Jesus is the good shepherd that gives life to the sheep. Because He is the good shepherd he will take care of you; the word says "you should take no thought for your life, what you shall eat; neither for the body, what you shall put on." ___Luke 12:22

"He makes me to lie down in green pastures, he leads me beside the still waters."

The word of God says that Jesus gives provision and peace. "I am the door, if by me any man enters in, he shall be saved and shall go in and out and find *pasture.*__John 10:9

"These things I have spoken unto you that in me you might have peace."—John 16:33

"He restores my soul; He leads me in the paths of righteousness for his name sake."

When you lose your way in the darkness of anger the shepherd leads you to safety. "All we like sheep have gone astray; we have turned every one to his own way." —Isaiah 53:6

"Yea though I walk through the valley of the shadow of death, I will fear no evil, for thou art with me, thy rod and thy staff they comfort me."

"He shall cover you with His feathers, and under His wings you shall take refuge; His truth shall be your shield and buckler. You shall not be afraid of the terror by night, nor of the arrow that flies by day, nor of the pestilence that walks in darkness, nor of the destruction that lays waste at noonday. A thousand may fall at your side, and ten thousand at your right hand; but it shall not come near you."—Psalm 91:4-7

"You prepare a table before me in the presence of mine enemies."

Who are your enemies? You may think of your enemies as people who are out to harm you, and you are correct; your enemies however, are not only limited to people. Many of you fight against invisible foes like: Alcoholism, drug addiction, anger, bitterness, anxiety and many other strongholds in your life. God prepared a table full of spiritual tools to be used in battle against your strongholds (enemies).

"For though we walk in the flesh, we do not war according to the flesh; For the weapons of our warfare are not carnal but mighty in God for pulling down strongholds, casting down arguments and every high thing that exalts itself against the knowledge of God, bringing every thought into captivity to the obedience of Christ." ___II Corinthians 10:3

God prepared a work table and set before you an assortment of weapons of warfare; according to Ephesians 6 you have at your disposal a complete armor: The belt of truth, the breastplate of righteousness, the preparation of the gospel of peace, the shield of faith, the helmet of salvation and the sword of the Spirit (which is the word of God).

"You anoint my head with oil, my cup runs over."

God anoints those He chooses to protect them from their enemies, "Do not touch my anointed ones, and do my prophets no harm." I Chronicles 16:22

"Surely goodness and mercy shall follow me all the days of my life, and I will dwell in the house of the Lord forever."

Goodness and mercy is found in the house of God; according to Matthew 6:33 you must seek the kingdom of God and all his righteousness, and these will be added to you.

My Journal Of
Things That Are True

Things That Are Noble

Truth

Giving

Wisdom

Ministry

Integrity

Forgiveness

Learning to receive

When you hear the word noble you may think of high moral standards, and you are correct. A person who is noble is held to a high standard, and is expected to take the high road; being noble however, does not mean being perfect.

Forgiveness

"In Him we have redemption through His blood, the forgiveness of sins, according to the riches of His grace."
__Ephesians 1:7

God sent His son to model forgiveness; no one is indebted to us as much as we are to God. If therefore, we have been forgiven much, can we forgive little?

"Bearing with one another, and forgiving one another, if anyone has a complaint against another; even as Christ forgave you, so you also must do." __Colossians 3:13

Sometimes the most difficult thing to do is ignore another's mistakes; you being perfect and not apt to make mistakes are able to forgive those who are less perfect.

"If my people who are called by my name will humble themselves, and pray and seek my face, and turn from their wicked ways, then I will hear from heaven, and will forgive their sin and heal their land." __II Chronicles 7:14

To ask for forgiveness, is to humble oneself and admit one's mistakes.

Forgiveness is not always easy; it may require you to tear down the shield of anger you use as protection. Good news! You don't have to do it all in one step, forgiveness is a process.

Step one: Think about it and practice forgiveness in your mind.

Step two: Rehearse it out loud.

Step three: Be accountable to someone else (let someone

know you are working on forgiveness, this provides accountability and decreases the likelihood of changing your mind).

Step four: Pray for strength to forgive. You must forgive others, according to Matthew 6:14 (For if you forgive men their trespasses, your heavenly Father will also forgive you).

Step five: Ask God to forgive you.

Step six: Forgive yourself.

At the end of this process, dispose of the IOU you have been holding on to for years. Once you forgive, the person owes you nothing; forgiveness is synonymous with PAID IN FULL!

Wisdom

"Happy is the man who finds wisdom, and the man who gains understanding; for her proceeds are better than the profits of silver, and her gain than fine gold. She is more precious than rubies, and all the things you may desire cannot compare with her." __Proverbs 3:13-15

By knowledge you may acquire riches, but it is by wisdom that you keep them.

"If any of you lacks wisdom, let him ask of God, who gives to all liberally and without reproach, and it will be given to him." __James 1:5

Wisdom is free and yours for the asking!

"Wisdom is better than strength." __Ecclesiastes 9:16

The energy required to maintain your anger and bitterness saps your strength; the wisdom of letting go of it, gives you strength.

Truth

"Lord, who may abide in your tabernacle? Who may dwell in your holy hill? He who walks uprightly, and works righteousness, and speaks the truth in his heart."
__Psalm 15:1-2

Speaking the truth is not always easy, but it is always the right thing!

"And you shall know the truth, and the truth shall make you free."

The lies you tell yourself to sustain bitter feelings are like shackles that bind you to the person you are bitter against; the truth is the key to free both.

"The entirety of your word is truth." __Psalm 119:160

Every aspect of the word of God is true!

Integrity

"Then the Lord said to Satan, Have you considered my servant Job? That there is non like him on the earth, a blameless and upright man, one who fears God and shuns evil; and still he holds fast to his integrity, although you incited me against him, to destroy him without cause." — Job 2:3

Showing integrity is not contingent on how you are treated! At times life seems unfair; you maybe the recipient of bad news or unfair treatment—illness, poverty—it begs the question why does bad things happen to good people? You may also wonder why be a person of integrity when the world does not seem to always honor it?

I participated in a celebration hosted by a few women in the church, appropriately called integra'tea. It is a yearly event in which women gather to worship God, have tea and fellowship. The purpose of the celebration is to honor women of integrity and encourage each other to be women of integrity; a scripture on the invitation caught my eye, because it answered the question—why have integrity when the world does not always seem to honor it? Matthew 5:14,16 reads, "You are the light of the world. A city that is set on a hill cannot be hidden; nor do they light a lamp and put it under a basket, but on a lamp stand, and it gives light to all who are in the house. So let your light shine before men, that they may see your good works and glorify your Father in heaven." The invitation also cited Psalms 7:8 "The Lord shall judge the people; judge me O Lord, according to my righteousness, and according to **my integrity** within me.

Although others may not always honor your sense of

integrity, God always honors it. You are the light of the world; your integrity sets the standard for others to follow, therefore let your integrity so shine that others may see it and glorify your father in heaven.

"The integrity of the upright will guide them, but the perversity of the unfaithful will destroy them." __Proverbs 11:3

If integrity is your guide you will not stumble when faced with hard decisions.

"In all things showing yourself to be a pattern of good works; in doctrine showing integrity, reverence, incorruptibility." __Titus 2:7

Integrity should be a pattern for your life.

Giving

"So let each one give as he purposes in his heart, not grudgingly or of necessity; for God loves a cheerful giver."
—II Corinthians 9:7

When you give of yourself grudgingly, you have not given you have taken.

"I am the good shepherd; the good shepherd gives His life for the sheep."
—John 10:11

The greatest example of a giver is Jesus; he gave the ultimate sacrifice.

"If you then, being evil, know how to give good gifts to your children, how much more will your Father who is in heaven give good things to those who ask Him!
—Matthew 7:11

Your heavenly father has gifts stored up for you.

My Journal Of Things That Are Noble

Things That Are Lovely

Best friends

Your soul mate

Family connections

Praying with someone

The Celebration of life

Holding the hand of an elderly person

Having a healthy relationship with someone is priceless; thinking about family or a friend, who have been there for you in your time of need, brings tears to your eyes and joy in your heart. Do you take your relationships for granted? Celebrating life is so much better, when someone is there to celebrate it with you.

Prayer

"Watch and pray, lest you enter into temptation. The spirit indeed is willing, but the flesh is weak." __Matthew 26:41

Prayer keeps you connected to the vine (Jesus) that provides the nutrients to the branches (Us).

**"...Pray for one another, that you may be healed. The effective, fervent prayer of a righteous man avails much."
__James 5:16**

Praying for others helps you to refocus; it gets you out of yourself to see the need around you.

"Be anxious for nothing, but in everything by prayer and supplication, with thanksgiving, let your requests be made known to God." __Philippians 4:6

The prayer of faith removes anxiety; when you pray, you turn the problem over to God.

Friends

"A friend loves at all times, and a bother is born for adversity." __Proverbs 17:17

True friends stick around during times of adversity and trials; true friendship is strengthened during hard times.

"A man who has friends must himself be friendly; there is a friend who sticks closer than a bother." __Proverbs 18:24

You cannot attract bees with vinegar; neither can you attract friends with a sour disposition.

"No longer do I call you servants, for a servant does not know what his master is doing; but I have called you friends, for all things that I heard from my Father I have made known to you." John 15:15

Jesus left us an example of true friendship.

"Two are better than one, because they have a good reward for their labor; for if they fall, one will lift up his companion; but woe to him who is alone when he falls, for he has no one to help him up." __Ecclesiastes 4:9-10

When the adversities of life knock you down, it is good to have a friend who can pick you back up.

"Though one may be overpowered by another, two can withstand him; and a threefold cord is not quickly broken."

You might be tempted to go it alone in life when things don't seem to go your way; remember, two can tackle a problem better than one!

Celebration Of Life

"And the Lord God formed man of the dust of the ground, and breathed into his nostrils the breath of life; and man became a living being." __Genesis 2:7

You are a living being! No longer dust, but made from dust; celebrate the moment life was breath into you.

"He will redeem their life from oppression and violence; and precious shall be their blood in His sight." __ Psalm72:14

The stress of daily living can be overwhelming; instead of something that is celebrated, life becomes something that is mourned.

"For whoever finds me finds life, and obtains favor from the Lord." __Proverbs 8:35

When you find the path to life, it calls for a celebration; even the angels in heaven celebrate the turning of one life to the Lord.

My Journal Of Things That Are Lovely

.

Things That Are Of Good Report

The gospel

Receiving healing

Giving someone good news

Living in harmony with your fellow man

God's word is the only report that promises eternal life!

The Gospel

""But they have not all obeyed the gospel. For Isaiah says, Lord, who has believed our report?" __Romans 10:16

We hear many reports in life—bad news from the doctor, a bad report card from school or a bad report on an inspection card at work. What better report than the gospel of good news. Do you believe God's report?

"...Repent and believe the gospel." __Mark 1:15

Turn around and believe the good news!

"In him you also trusted, after you heard the word of truth, the gospel of your salvation; in whom also, having believed, you were sealed with the Holy Spirit of promise." __Ephesians 1:13

It is by hearing the gospel that you come to know Christ and believe in him.

Healing

"Have mercy on me, O Lord, for I am weak; Lord heal me for my bones are troubled." __Psalm 6:1

When you think of healing do you thing of physical healing alone? The need for spiritual healing can cause physical and psychological problems.

"The spirit of the Lord is upon me, because he has anointed me to preach the gospel to the poor. He has sent me to heal the brokenhearted, to preach deliverance to the captives and recovery of sight to the blind, to set at liberty those who are oppressed." __Luke 4:18

The word of God provides healing for all parts of you; body, mind, and spirit.

"Bless the Lord, o my soul, and forget not all his benefits: Who forgives all your iniquities, who heals all your diseases." __Psalm 103:3

God heals it all!

My Journal Of
Things That Are Of Good Report

POEMS FOR THE SOUL

***

Thanks
By: Allison Chambers Coxsey

All my life I kept my dreams,
Tucked somewhere deep inside;
Till one by one you pulled them out,
With nothing left to hide.
You pointed to my deepest dreams,
You told me I should try;
Then gently told me I had wings,
And showed me how to fly.
Then somehow you reached in my heart,
Made words flow like a stream;
With loving inspiration,
You became part of the dream.
I never would have dreamed my dreams,
They never would have come true;
Those dreams would not be realized,
If God had not sent you.

Footprints
Author Unknown

One night a man had a dream.
He dreamed he was walking
Along the beach
With the Lord.
Across the sky flashed
Scenes from his life.
For each scene
He noticed two sets
Of footprints in the sand;
One belonged to him,
And the other to the Lord.
When the last scene of
His life flashed before him,
He looked back at the
Footprints in the sand.
He noticed that many
Times along the path
Of his life there was
Only on set of footprints.
He also noticed that
It happened at the very
Lowest and saddest
Times in his life.
This really bothered him
And he questioned
The Lord about it.
"Lord, you said
That once I decided
To follow you, you'd walk

With me all the way.
But I have noticed that
At the worst time in my life,
There is only one
Set of footprints.
How could you leave me when
I needed you the most?
The Lord replied
"My precious,
Precious child,
I love you and would
Never leave you.
During your
Times of suffering
And when you see only
One set of footprints,
It was then that I carried you."

The Cross Room
Author Unknown

The young man was at the end of his rope.
Seeing no way out, he dropped to his knees in prayer.
"Lord, I can't go on," he said.
"I have too heavy a cross to bear."
The Lord replied,
"My son, if you can't bear its weight,
Just place your cross inside this room.
Then open another door
And pick any cross you wish."
The man was filled with relief.
"Thank you, Lord,"
He sighed, and did as he was told.
As he looked around the room
He saw many different crosses;
Some so large the tops were not visible.
Then he spotted a tiny cross
Leaning against a far wall.
"I'd like that one, Lord,"
He whispered. And the Lord replied,
"My son, that's the cross you brought in."

Unforgiveness
By: Allison Chambers Coxsey

Nothing is as painful
As unforgiveness to the soul;
A heart that's torn asunder,
With forgiveness becomes whole.
A single kind word spoken
Means more than countless words;
The three words, "I forgive you,"
Are all the need be heard.
To a soul that has been wounded,
Like a healing, cooling balm;
Forgiveness soothes and comforts,
Till at last the soul is calm.
For the soul that seeks forgiveness,
When forgiveness can't be found;
It struggles vainly everyday,
To hear that simple sound.
The power in those three kind words,
Can heal a heart that's broken;
But that heart cannot begin to heal,
As long as words remain unspoken.
Compassion in it's purest sense,
Reside in those three words;
The three words, "I forgive you,"
Are all that need be heard.

Blessings
Author Unknown

I knelt to pray when day was done
And prayed, "O Lord, bless everyone,
Lift from each saddened heart the pain
And let the sick be well again."
And then I woke another day
The whole daylong I did not try
To wipe a tear from any eye.
I did not try to share the load
Of any brother on the road.
I did not even go to see
The sick man just next door to me.
Yet once again when day was done
I prayed, "O Lord, bless everyone."
But as I prayed, into my ear
There came a voice that whispered clear,
"Pause now, my son, before you pray.
Whom have you tried to bless today?
God's sweetest blessing always go
By hands that serve him here below."
And then I hid my face and cried,
"Forgive me, God, I have not tried,
But let me live another day
And I will live the way I pray."

Heart Prints
Author Unknown

Whatever our hands touch...
We leave fingerprints!
On walls, on furniture,
On doorknobs, dishes, books,

As we touch we leave our identity.
Oh please where ever I go today,
Help me leave heart prints!
Heart prints of compassion
Of understanding and love.
Heart prints of kindness
And genuine concern.

May my heart touch a lonely neighbor
Or a runaway daughter,
Or an anxious mother,
Or, perhaps, a dear friend!

I shall go out today
To leave heart prints,
And if someone should say
"I felt your touch,"
May that one sense be...

YOUR LOVE
Touching through
Me.

To Journey With Jesus
By: Karla W. Daigle

Oh, to have been there
When our Savior was conceived.
When the Glory of God descended
Upon the woman who had believed
That she would bear the King of Kings,
The Son of our Heavenly Father.

Oh, to have been with Mary,
Our gracious Redeemer's mother.
Oh, to have been there
When she wrapped the Holy babe,
To have felt His glowing presence
In the manger where He lay.
To have seen God's love shining
From heaven's dawning morn.

Oh, to have worshipped Jesus
From the moment that He was born!
Oh, to have been there
When the thousands gathered 'round
For as He taught His holy message,
They uttered not a sound.
Oh, to have seen the miracles
That the Messiah had performed
Where He healed the sick, raised the dead
And calmed the violent storm.

Oh, to have been there
When they sentenced Him to die.

When they mocked and persecuted Him.
And their Master, the disciples denied.
Oh, to have seen Him struggle
With the burden of the cross.
This, our Savior lovingly endured
To redeem the sinners yet lost.

Oh, to have been there
When He gave His life that day.
When at Calvary, He suffered a death
That would wipe our sins away.
Oh, to have grieved with Mary
As she laid her son to rest
And as she wrapped the Holy shroud
'Round the man who'd fulfilled his quest.

Oh, to have been there
When the stone was rolled aside
To bring forth our risen Savior
So that forever, He could guide!
The Son of God had come to earth
To die for all who believe.
Oh, to respond to the heavenly trumpets
When His flock, our Shepherd retrives!

Your Soul Mate

The Shulamite Woman Seeks Her Lover
—Song of Solomon 3

"By night on my bed I
Sought the one I love;
I sought him,
But I did not find him.
I will rise not, I said,
And go about the city.
In the streets and in the
Squares I will seek
The one I love.
I sought him,
But I did not find him.
The watchmen who go
About the city found me,
To whom I said,
Have you seen the one I love?
Scarcely had I passed by them,
When I found the one I love.
I held him and would not let him go,
Until I had brought him
To the house of my mother,
And into the chamber of
Her who conceived me."

Your Soul Mate

A Poem To His Beloved
__Song of Solomon 4

"Behold, you are fair, my love!
Behold, you are fair.
You have dove's eyes
Behind your veil.
Your hair is like
A flock of goats,
Going down from
Mount Gilead.
Your teeth are like
A flock of shorn sheep,
Which have come up
From the washing.
Every one of
Which bears twins,
And none is
Barren among them.
Your lips are like
A strand of scarlet,
And your mouth is lovely.
Your temples behind your
Veil are like a piece
Of pomegranate.
Your neck is like
The tower of David,
Built for an armory on
Which hand a

Thousand buckler,
All shields of mighty men.
Your two breasts
Are like two fawns,
Twins of a gazelle,
Which feed among the lilies.
Until the day breaks
And the shadows flee away,
I will go my way to
The mountain of myrrh
And to the hill
Of frankincense.
You are all fair my love
And there is no spot in you.
Come with me
From Lebanon,
My spouse,
With me from Lebanon.
Look from the top of Amana,
From the top of
Senir and Hermo.
From the lion's dens,
From the mountains
Of the leopards.
You have ravished my heart,
My sister, my spouse;
You have ravished my heart
With one look of your eyes,
With one link of your necklace;
How fair is your love,
My sister, my spouse!
How much better
Than wine is your love,
And the scent of
Your perfumes
Than all spices!
Your lips, O my spouse,

Drip as the honeycomb;
Honey and milk **are**
Under your tongue;
And the fragrance of
Your garments is
Like the fragrance
Of Lebanon.
A garden enclosed
Is my sister,
My spouse;
A spring shut up,
A fountain sealed.
Your plants are an orchard
Of pomegranates
With pleasant fruits;
Fragrant henna
With spikenard
And saffron,
calamus and cinnamon,
With all trees
Of frankincense,
Myrrh and aloes,
With all the chief spices;
A well of living waters,
And streams from Lebanon.

No Prayer Goes Unheard
By Helen Steiner Rice

Often we pause and wonder
When we kneel down to pray
Can God really hear
The prayers that we say....
But if we keep praying
And talking to Him,
He'll brighten the soul
That was clouded and dim,
And as we continue
Our burden seems lighter,
Our sorrow is softened
And our outlook is brighter
For though we feel helpless
And alone when we start,
Our prayer is the key
That opens the heart,
And as our heart opens
The dear Lord comes in
And the prayer that we felt
We could never begin
Is so easy to say
For the Lord understands
And gives us new strength
By the touch of His hands.

The Place Of Meditation
By Helen Steiner Rice

So we may know God better
And feel His quiet power,
Let us daily keep in silence
A Meditation Hour—
For to understand God's greatness
And to use His gifts each day
The soul must learn to meet Him
In a meditative way,
For our Father tells His children
That if they would know His will
They must seek Him in the silence
When all is calm and still...
For nature's greatest forces
Are found in quiet things
Like softly falling snowflakes
Drifting down on angel's wings,
Or petals dropping soundlessly
From a lovely full-blown rose,
So God comes closest to us
When our souls are in repose...

I Want To Set Your Soul Free
By Robin Gorley

I want to set your soul free
To soar, to see, to feel
With the wind, the sun
Run with the elements

I want to soothe your tired body
With my touch
To smooth your wrinkled brow
To sprinkle angel dust in your eyes
And roses in your cheeks

My Soul Is Filled
By Robin Gorley

Music fills my soul
Leaving many impressions
Upon my body
My whole life has
Been surrounded by
The flow of music trends
As I fill my days
With the sound
Of music, I'll remember
Those who have put my
Dreams together.
My soul is filled.

Something's About To Happen
By Ronald Veazie

Something's about to happen
'Cause every time you're near
My heart begins to flutter
And my eyes begin to tear

Something's about to happen
'Cause when I think of you
All my blues fly away
And my dreams begin to come true

Something's about to happen
'Cause when I hold your hand
I begin to dream
That I could be your man

Something's about to happen
'Cause every time I hear
Your sweet and gently voice
My life becomes so clear

Something's about to happen
I know that this is true
This feeling I have is called love
This feeling I have is you

A Miracle
By Robin Gorley

We are, each of us, a miracle
Unique in our own way
Each day is made special
By what we bring to it
The joy, the caring, and the closeness we share,
We explore our differences
And become closer to each other
As we celebrate the
Gift of this miracle
Our life, a miracle to us.

My Mother
By Ronald Veazie

I came into this world
Through the miracle of birth
My mother carried me
For nine months on this earth
Before I actually got here
She prayed to God for me
That I would be healthy

Wealthy, wise and able to clearly see
She sacrificed so much
To make my world so grand
In hopes I would be strong
And always able to stand

My mother used to walk a mile
With a basket full of clothes
To make sure I was clean
In the morning when I arose
With a third grade education
She taught me so much about life
Things I could never learn in school
Or even from my wife

Her fortitude and grit
Are qualities I admire
It taught me to never quit
And to make it through the fire

I know that God will bless her
In her eternal home
Where she deserves great rewards
And to never be alone
My mother means so much to me
And she will always know
The lessons she has taught me
That has caused my life to grow

On The Wings Of A Prayer
By Helen Steiner Rice

Just close your eyes
And open your heart,
And feel your worries
And cares depart.
Just yield yourself
To the Father above,
And let him hold you
Secure in his love.

For life on earth grows
More involved,
With endless problems
That can't be solved,
But God only ask
Us to do our best,
Then he will take over
And finish the rest...

So when you are tired,
Discouraged and blue,
There is always one door
That is open to you,
And that is the door to
The House of Prayer,
And you'll find God
Waiting to meet you there.
And The House of Prayer
Is no further away,
Than the quiet spot
Where you kneel and pray.

For the heart is a temple
When God is there
As we place ourselves
In his loving care.
And he hears every prayer
And answers each one
When we pray in His name
Thy will be done.
The burdens that seemed
Too heavy to bear
Are lifted away on
The wings of a prayer.

SHE!
By Nola Veazie

Who is she?
A woman saved by grace;
Not much to look at
Yet pleasing to the eyes;
She is old and young in her spirit,
Trapped and free.
She is sad and joyful,
The woman is me.
You are fearfully
And wonderfully made,
I formed you in
Your mother's womb,
Your thoughts
I know very well,
Said her maker.
I infused the
Breath of life in you
And placed
in you my lamp
To illuminate
the secret places
In your heart.
Who are you
Asked her maker?
The world said SHE!
Little does
The world know
Who I really am;
Little did I

Know who I was.
I can give you
The details of my life,
The places I've been,
The people I've seen;
I don't know if I can tell you
The reason for my being.
Life doesn't
always seem fair,
But I believe it is;
It may not always be equitable,
But it's fairness lies
In the inequality that makes you
Who you are suppose to be.
So many stories about me,
Telling of my disgrace;
The man who violated me,
The one who left;
The mother who rejected me,
The sister I wish I could be.
I'm glad life doesn't always
End the way it begins,
It offers an
Opportunity for change;
If life negated you
The opportunity
For change,
Then you still
Would be SHE!
This story is yours,
It offers you a chance
To water the
Seed planted in you,
A chance to pull the weeds
That threatens to
Choke and kill the seed.

The Serenity Prayer
By Reinhold Niebuhr (1892-1971)

God, grant me the serenity
To accept the things
I cannot change,
Courage to change the
Things I can,
And the Wisdom
To know the difference.

Living one day at a time;
Enjoying one moment at a time;
Accepting hardship as the
Pathway to peace.

Taking, as He did, this
Sinful world as it is,
Not as I would have it.

Trusting that He will make
All things right if I
Surrender to his will;

That I may be reasonably happy
In this life, and supremely
Happy with Him forever in
The next.

The information contained in this book is not a substitution for professional or pastoral counseling. Unregulated anger can cripple your life, causing spiritual and emotional paralysis. If you are suffering from depression or anxiety as a result of your anger, seek counseling immediately.

ABOUT THE AUTHOR

Nola Veazie is a retired Air Force veteran who spent the last 13 years of her military career in the Mental Health/ Substance Abuse career field, as Superintendent for the Medical Operations Squadron. Nola is the CEO of V-Solutions Consulting, a company that provides consulting services for Drug and Alcohol programs, group homes and other Non-Profit Mental Health and Drug and Alcohol organizations. She led Stress and Anger management groups in the Federal Prison system, in addition to Relapse Prevention, Parenting, and Relationship classes.

This author has written a number of articles on Relapse Prevention, Depression and other Mental Health issues. She has also authored the book Relapse Prevention 101: The Dawn of Sobriety, an innovative approach to Relapse Prevention.